THE IMMIGRANTS

THE
IMMIGRANTS
Gloria Montero

James Lorimer & Company, Publishers
Toronto 1977

ISBN 0-88862-146-9 Cloth
　　　　0-88862-147-7 Paper

Cover design: Don Fernley
Cover photograph: Vincent Marchese

6 5 4 3 2 1　　77 78 79 80 81 82

James Lorimer & Company, Publishers
Egerton Ryerson Memorial Building
35 Britain Street
Toronto, Ontario

Printed and bound in Canada

Canadian Cataloguing in Publication Data

Montero, Gloria, 1933-
　The immigrants

ISBN 0-88862-146-9

1. Canada – Foreign population.　2. Canada –
Emigration and immigration.　I. Title.

FC104.M65　301.32'4'0971　C77-001395-3
F1035.A1M65

Contents

I'll never forget my first years here. I was an unknown person among unknown people.

Taki, restaurant owner

We wouldn't come, you know, if there was enough bread in our own countries. We just wouldn't come. Isn't hunger as good a reason for immigration as anything else? Only hunger drives us here.

Julia, rubber factory worker

The early experiences you have as an immigrant are like experiences in the war. They are not all pleasant while you go through them, but afterwards you wouldn't change a thing. What's more, they give you a kind of strength.

Dorothy, housewife

You miss your own people when you come here. It's something you never think about before you come. It's something you could not imagine until you are here and the loneliness takes you over.

Pete, technician

When I first came here I wanted to be absorbed. It was almost an act of amputation I wanted to commit. I needed so much to be accepted as a Canadian.

Marlène, unemployed

Acknowledgments

This kind of book can be written only with the help of many people. My heartfelt thanks first of all to the men, women and children who shared their lives with me and spent long hours telling me their stories. My gratitude also to all the good friends who helped me meet so many people and whose warm hospitality made me welcome in every part of the country. To Jim Lorimer my thanks for the new, wider perspective he added. Finally, to David my special thanks for believing in this book long before it became a reality.

G. M.

For Trini, my grandmother,
who taught me about courage
and about laughter

Preface

This is a book about men and women vital to the fabric of this country. A number of them came here many years ago. Some of them are newcomers. Most are hardly known beyond their own streets or work places. All of them have chosen Canada as their home; and these are their stories, their perceptions, their hopes, their humiliations, their disappointments, their achievements, their dreams.

The idea for the book grew out of my involvement with other immigrants at the Centre for Spanish-speaking Peoples in Toronto. Over the years, I met so many remarkable people whose potential was strangled in the day-to-day battle for existence, the wranglings with bureaucracy, the painful coming to terms with a strange, new culture.

Immigration is a prime topic of discussion in Canada, but we always talk *about* immigrants. I felt it was time to redress the balance. The other side of the story needed telling. So I set off with my tape recorder to ask immigrants to talk about their lives. I spent two years travelling across Canada talking to people. Slowly I began to realize that this book had begun many, many years before.

I grew up in Australia in a small, tropical town close by the fabled Barrier Reef. My family were immigrants from Asturias, in the north of Spain. I learned English, I went to school, yet always I felt that somehow I was different. I belonged to a family which was patently unlike the families of my friends. The differences were not always tangible, but they were very real. No one else that I knew had a grandmother who would ride on a bus and get acquainted with almost every other passenger by the time she had reached her stop.

Our house was a meeting place for all the Spanish immigrants in town. They drank wine and talked politics for hours on end. At school, a different cultural background was not seen as an advantage. There was no recognition of what I might have experienced. Many things that were unfamiliar to me were given an importance I found difficult to understand.

How many times I wished my family could be rich and English. It seemed it must be easier to live that way. But I never talked about these feelings. I felt guilty and ambivalent, and I compensated by being clever at school. I loved my family dearly. I knew they were special people. What's more, our family picnics and dinners were a lot more exciting than those of any of my friends. Still, to a child wanting desperately to be accepted, it was hard to grow up feeling so different. I was 16 years old before I came to fully accept who I was.

So many details of those years – uncertainties, hurts, frustrations – swept back over me as I talked to people for this book. They told me of incidents in their own lives very similar to things I had experienced myself. Perhaps my own identification with the women, the men and the children I talked to made it easier for me to intrude on their lives, to urge them to tell me stories they sometimes preferred to forget.

There were a lot of tears shed in the telling of these stories. But there was laughter, too. Surprisingly, the obvious problems of language presented the easiest hurdle. When it was difficult for a person to talk comfortably in English and we had another common language, we would use that. On a few occasions, we talked with the help of a friend who made it easy to jump back and forth from English to Japanese, Punjabi or whatever.

Some people had no trouble talking about themselves. A number were genuinely amazed that anyone would think them important enough to want to know their stories. More than a few were afraid they might be recognized. They would talk only if their names were not used. It was important that employers, husbands, mothers or sisters-in-law were not able to identify them. That is why I have used only first names. I have included occupations simply as a way of introducing a little more of the milieu of people's daily lives. Many probably have changed jobs since we talked. Some no doubt are out of work. A few lucky ones might now be doing what they were trained to do.

No one is identified by ethnic background. Often this comes out in the story. I found that ethnicity is not what determines how well an immigrant lands on his or her feet in Canada. A ruthless economic system dispenses quickly with such differences. What's more, many of the difficulties encountered by immigrants are identical to the serious problems lived each day by Canada's Indian and Inuit people, by Canadian migrant workers and mothers on welfare.

Though I tried to cover as broad a spectrum as possible in talking to immigrants, my selection of people was quite random. Someone would know "an interesting woman who used to work in a factory making tents." Or perhaps the mechanic at the corner garage was from "some foreign place." Each time I reached a new town one contact would lead to another and another. And so it went on. At the end of two years, I had spoken to more than 400 people. They ranged in age from 4 to 84; they came from every corner of the globe and had lived in all of Canada's 10 provinces.

Not all the stories I gathered are included here, but they all form the basis of this book. Naturally, a selection had to be made from the vast amount of material recorded. No individual story presumes to represent the experience of any particular ethnic group. What is presented here is the collective story of Canada's immigrants as it was told to me in towns, cities and hamlets from one end of the country to the other.

The book is divided into seven sections, with a short introduction and conclusion. Three of these sections, Parts I, IV and VII, are made up of longer personal histories. The other four sections are made up of thematic chapters which draw together brief passages from conversations I had with many of the other people. Part II examines the whole area of work – finding a job (or not being able to get one), joining a union and searching for ways to fulfill one's potential. Part III explains what it is like to settle into a strange, new culture, trying to cope with an unfamiliar world of large, impersonal institutions. Part V is devoted to the immigrant's social world – stories of relationships between friends, lovers, children and families. Part VI looks at the broader picture of what it means to be a Canadian.

I hope that these stories will help us to know each other better. For all our differences we are amazingly similar. Our common needs as citizens of an industrial Canada trying to cope with inflation, unemployment and pollution make our backgrounds singularly unimportant. Now that we make our homes in Canada, we are Canadian. And a Canadian, I have learned, wears a wide array of skin colours, speaks in a fascinating range of accents, has a collective life experience that spans all cultures, all continents. This, surely, gives this country a special strength.

Canadian society is smug about the advantages it offers immigrants. But immigration is a two-way street and the country gains as much as the individual who comes here. Often, the country gains considerably more.

For me, the Canadians represented here have been a great lesson. They have given me something of their strength, their compassion, their humour and their wisdom. With this book I thank them.

G. M.

Introduction:
You don't let go

What does it mean to become an immigrant, to leave a whole world behind and come to terms with a new one? Though each person's experience is different, there are emotions that are common to all.

Goodbye

I am settled here now. When I came, I came forever. Before I left Italy I took a day and went out with my dog. I said, "Goodbye mountains, I don't know if I will ever see you again. Goodbye, river. Goodbye, city." I really left. My husband didn't do that. He didn't really leave emotionally. For the first year he was neither here nor there.

Antonia, day care supervisor

Shouting at you

I can talk to you now, but when I first came here eight years ago I knew "yes" and "no" and what they meant. Whenever I'd go into a store there would be a tight knot inside me in case I could not handle the exchange with the person serving me. I remember once going into a government office where I had to fill out a form. There were all sorts of questions. Answer yes or no, fill in the box, leave this blank. I became so confused. I didn't know what to answer yes or no to. I wrote in the part where I should have left it blank. I didn't understand even the simplest things. It just got worse and worse until I tore it up and ran out crying.

When I look back on those first years and the big, big problem of language, I think that big knot inside me dominated my whole life.

13

And to make it worse, people here tend to shout at you to get you to understand English. They seem to think that the louder they shout, the better you'll be able to understand.

Adriana, housewife

Not good inside

It was hard in the beginning. The kids at school didn't really know me as yet. The first day of school we were all friends together, then after a while they separated and went back into their own friendships again. I got some friends now though, some good friends.

They started calling me names at first 'cause of my colour. Then they stopped. It wasn't too much of a shock to me though. Once in a while it had happened to me in Jamaica. You get used to lots of different things. But even after they stopped, whenever I'd do something to them, they'd start to call me names. It made me feel not good inside. I pretty well work it out though. It doesn't worry me too much.

I think Canada is a nice place to live. I like it, though I don't like it when it's very, very cold. I knew my mom had to leave us and come to work here to get a place and all. It felt funny when I was first back with my mom. It's hard to talk about it.

Kirk, 13 years old

Underdeveloped

Many Canadians seem to think that if a person comes from an underdeveloped country, she must be underdeveloped too.

Beatriz, education worker

Hi

My first Christmas here, I went to International Christmas in Truro. It had been hard to make friends here because of the language, but after the first couple of days in Truro I became very confident and much more sure of myself. I started to have a better feeling about everybody. One evening I was with some friends I had just met at a party. We decided to go and walk around the town to see what was going on. Everyone looked friendly, maybe because it was Christmas. We looked at the shops. It was around 9 or 10 in the evening. A few guys passed us in the street. I said "Hi" to them. It is our way. In Afghanistan, we are very open to people.

These guys stopped and said something to me but I didn't understand what they were saying. I still had a language problem. My friends who were probably more experienced, they ran away. But I didn't. I stayed there. I started again to try to talk to them, to say "Hi" and "Merry Christmas," and they began to hit me and beat me up. They broke my arm and I ended up spending that first Christmas here in hospital. I guess I was stunned. I have never hit anyone in my life and it was the first time anyone had ever hit me. I wasn't angry. I'm not sure why I wasn't, but I thought somehow it was probably my own fault. Those guys didn't know me and I told them "Hi." They answered my "Hi" in their way.

Amin, student

Dirt

It's all right now. We're doing all right. But we have worked hard and we sacrificed many things. And if you want to do it, you can get ahead. But the ones that are coming now, they don't want to be treated like dirt. They expect to be treated like real Canadians from the first day. They have to learn that it doesn't happen that way. You take the dirt and you take the low jobs, but you don't let go. And after a few years, you have proved you are as good as they are. When you've got money, too, then they start to show you respect. A lot of blacks and Colombians, even the Italians coming now, they want it easy. It doesn't happen that way, if you are an immigrant.

Mariana, restaurant owner

I

SEVEN LIVES

1 Hatsue:
A picture bride

"In 1958, I came here as a picture bride," she says smiling. Then adds with a twinkle in her eye, "That's very Japanese, eh?" Warm and witty, Hatsue impresses me as being a thoroughly modern Canadian woman in outlook. But she assures me that there are some differences. "In Japan, women have to be subservient to the man. I still follow that. I wanted to go above my husband but he wouldn't even let me be equal. He was fairly old when we were married so he had rigid ideas about family relationships. But in any case, I see many women here who are not subservient to their husbands and it does not seem to make them any happier."

My first husband died during the Second World War. My son had never known his father and now he was 17 and my own father convinced me I should marry again. Friends of my family had this relative in Canada. My picture was sent to him and he wrote and asked me to marry him. I came alone a year before my son and I felt very scared. On the boat with me were five other women who were also coming as "picture brides."

I was 36 years old and I had only been married for six months when my husband was torpedoed in the war, so many years before. I was living in Hiroshima with my son and on August 5, 1945, we went to the country to visit my parents. The next day, at 8 o'clock in the morning, the city was destroyed by the atomic bomb. Our house was completely burned to the ground. If we had been there we would have both been killed. We lived then on the farm with my parents for 15 years while my son was growing up, until I came to Canada.

I spoke no English and when I arrived I wanted to go straight back to Japan. I thought that my husband looked better in his picture than in real life. However he was very kind. He was 51 years old. He came to meet me and we were married, but after a week he had to go back to Prince George where he was working in a sawmill. He left me with relatives in Vancouver for three months. I was trying to learn English and get used to all the new things here. In my country I had never eaten bread, only rice, but here people eat bread every day. And even now I don't like bread.

My head was full of confusion. There was so much to get used to – the new language, new food, new customs and even the fact that I was married again after so many years to a man I scarcely knew. After three months I joined my husband in a little house in Prince George. It was bitterly cold with snow many feet high all around. There were no other Japanese living there but us, so it was very frightening. Life there was very different from what I had expected. There was no electric light, no running water. We had to carry the water from the river.

When my son came the next year he and my husband didn't get on together. He refused to call my husband "Papa" and used to cry all the time. It made me very sad, so I sent him to school in Vancouver. Then I became pregnant and had a little girl. After the birth I had a nervous breakdown. I couldn't get used to the new life and there was no one to talk to. I worried about my son and about the new baby. Finally, some white neighbours took care of my daughter and I was sent down to hospital in Vancouver. For five years I was back and forth, in and out of hospital and then I seemed to be all right. I had several miscarriages after that and eventually came to Vancouver with my daughter. I tried very hard all this time to learn English. I would write down Japanese words and phrases and then write down the English and try to learn it. I was doing housework for $1.25 an hour and even here my poor English made it difficult. Then I got seasonal work in the cannery.

Now my life is good. I am happy and all my problems are over. When my husband retired he joined us in Vancouver. My son is married to a nice Japanese girl and my daughter is now 15. She is in grade 12 and wants to go on to university. I want her to study more. She is a good student and speaks both Japanese and English very well. It was good I was patient in the beginning and didn't go back to Japan. I think this country's life is easier. I would still like to speak better English, but I am too old now. Still I am very happy here. I have a good life.

Hatsue, fish cannery worker

2 Emmy: This is my country now

We sit in the kitchen. At the window, green plants thrive in the clear Alberta sunshine and spill over the painted cans that serve as pots. The room is spacious and serene. That's the feeling I get from the woman, too. Her large hands serve me endless cups of good, strong coffee and slices of a delicious nut bread.

I am here 16 years. Only 46 years ago was I born and 16 of them now I have been in Canada. Yet I feel my bones are shaped the Canadian way, shaped by the prairie winter, by the air of the springtime, by the western sun in summer.

I came from Austria. It was very hard in Europe after the Second World War. I lived for some time in Frankfurt and then I was in Bonn. I worked in small offices. I was what you might call a secretary. But that was a grand name for the little girl that got the coffee, bought the newspapers, answered the telephone and typed some letters. My family was destroyed by the war. One of my sisters had gone to England and was married there to an Englishman. We were separated many years, only sending each other Christmas cards or maybe a letter for a birthday. Several times she asked that I consider going there to live with her, but inside me was restless. I felt that if I should make a new life, it should be on a soil far away in a new land.

Looking back I realized now that I knew little of the country, but it seemed a way of ensuring something different, something to wipe away all the pain of the years before. Through another person in the office where I worked I had met a Canadian couple. I spoke with them only once or twice but there was something in their manner which was very appealing to me. I met them three or four years before I decided to come to Canada, but I remembered always that they came from Calgary, Alberta. And so when at the immigration office I was asked where I would like to settle in Canada, I said "Alberta. Calgary, Alberta."

At school I had learnt some English and then for six months before I left I took evening classes in the language. That helped me, I suppose, but still it did not exactly prepare me for the strangeness of the accents I heard when I reached Calgary. I had thought of being able to work in another small office here, but the language was very difficult for me, and everyone seemed to speak so quickly. I was lost.

However, people were friendly and most of them were patient with me, too. They spoke slowly when I asked and repeated words or even whole phrases until I understood. I asked at a restaurant for work. They had nothing, but a woman there gave me the name of a house where a family needed someone to clean. Those days I made only $7 a day, and I could find work only for three days a week. I had brought very little money with me and by the end of three months, even by living frugally, I had almost no money left. Still, I was optimistic. I loved the land and felt a strong affinity for the kind of people I met here.

One night a family I had met, a Dutch family whose parents had come to Canada many years before, asked me to go with them to visit some friends on a farm outside the city. It was the end of April, I remember, and the land was just warming after the winter. The farmer was of Ukrainian parentage and his wife was Dutch. They had two daughters and one son – a young man strong and straight like a tree. We talked together a great deal that night and he promised to see me in Calgary the next weekend. It was an exciting time for me. Four months later we were married. I could hardly believe it. I had been alone for so many years, working and taking care of myself. It seemed a miracle that now there was someone beside me.

The first six years after our marriage we lived on the farm and worked very hard. They were good years. I felt then I learned what

Canada was. A country has its own personality, and I felt I grew intimately acquainted with this personality of western Canada. I was very happy. We had little money, but it was a good feeling to be part of a family again, to belong somewhere. However, the farm could not sustain us all and my husband and I moved away. He became a carpenter. It was pretty slow in the beginning, but I worked as a cook in a local hotel and we managed to get on our feet after a little while. And finally, we built our own house.

We would have liked a child, but no child came to us. So we thought of adoption. I wanted to give warmth and a family to someone, as it had been given to me. Now we have two boys who will grow up, I think, like my husband strong and husky. We are a family. A Canadian family. This is my country now. There is no doubt of it at all.

Emmy, housewife

3 Angela:
Alone in Canada

Angela and I met many times before she would agree to tell me her story. "I am a woman. Nothing more," she said once. "I am not too interesting." I tell her that my book will be a collection of the stories of women and men. Nothing more. She smiles then, but there is no laughter in her dark eyes.

I miss my children so much that sometimes I just lie in bed with their pictures in my hands and cry. It is now eight months since I came here from Guatemala. That's a long time when you are only four years old, or three, or nearly two like my little Juanito. Do they remember their mother?

I was a hairdresser in my country, but it is very difficult for work there and after a while I lost my job and just used to work at home doing the hair of my two cousins and some neighbour women on my street. I didn't make very much money because often they could not pay me, but I would still do their hair. One of my cousins was a young widow and she had this boyfriend that wanted to marry her but would never say exactly when. So she always wanted to look pretty. And then my neighbours would say, "We'll pay you when we can. You know that." I knew that the way we all were they would never pay me. But I liked to work too. I would have liked more to work outside and bring in some real money but . . . .

Then things got bad in the mill where my husband worked. For three months he was laid off. It was very hard then. We had no money after the first two months and very little food. You don't mind for yourself, but for your children your heart breaks. Then somebody from my town spoke of Canada. He had been here for nearly two years working in Montreal. He spoke so much of the big money and the good opportunities. At first my husband wanted to borrow the money and come, but then his mill started up again and he went back to work. But we kept talking about Canada.

After a while I began to feel that I should be the one to come to Canada. I thought about it for a long time before I said anything to my husband. I didn't think he would want me to come by myself. But the more I thought about it, the more sensible it seemed. Just for a while to make some money, and then he would come and bring the children. The longer I thought about it, the better I felt. I would be the one, for a while at least, to bring in the real money in the family.

One night I mentioned it to my husband. I was not prepared for his reaction. He thought it was a good idea. I felt good and strong inside. We worked out a plan for the children. One of my cousins would stay in the house and mind them because my mother is too old now and not very well.

We had a big party in my house the night before I left. I think it was only then I really began to think that it would be hard to come and leave the little ones and my husband, too. We all cried a bit the day I left. Even my husband.

I didn't know too much about Canada. I didn't know French. I didn't know English. I couldn't understand anything at the airport. For five hours I had to wait until they brought someone to translate for me and tell me that they wanted to deport me and send me back to Guatemala. I was very frightened. I felt I was in jail. They wouldn't let me out of this room. I cried, I am ashamed to say. I don't know why, but because I was there alone without my husband and the children, I felt I should not have cried. But all the emotion of the past days and leaving the family and the journey itself had made me tired and nervous. I explained that we had had to borrow part of the money for my journey and that I only wanted to try to work here for a little while. Then I would go back to my family.

I still don't understand exactly what happened because the man who was translating for me did not seem to understand either exactly what was going on. I don't know who he was. I have a feeling that he was another passenger going somewhere or coming from somewhere who just came to help out. But perhaps that is wrong. He didn't talk too much to me. In fact, when I stopped crying and took some notice of him I had the feeling he was scared, too. He told me I must not say I wanted to work but just that I was a tourist and I wanted to visit Canada.

The immigration man said I did not have enough money to stay here. But I told him that some people from my town were here and that I would be with them, so I would not need too much money. I did have the address of a woman that was known to the friend of my husband's who had lived here. I was allowed to stay as a tourist for three months. The man who was translating for me phoned the woman and she told me to wait at the airport. She sent her son-in-law to get me in his car. I was tired, but I remember all the lights of the city as we came in. It looked very pretty and I felt that maybe it was going to be all right.

For three months I seemed to have good luck. The woman's brother owned a restaurant and he gave me a work offer. In about a month, Immigration gave me a work permit. But only for three months. Then I would have to go back and have it renewed. I thought I was going to be a waitress in the restaurant, but he said first I should get some experience and learn some French, so he started me off in the kitchen. I worked hard and I worked many hours overtime in that place. I was grateful for the help they gave me. I didn't learn any French, but I didn't care much about that. I had most of my meals in the restaurant kitchen and I could save almost everything I earned.

At the end of three months, the restaurant owner told me he would help me get my tourist card renewed. And he did. I was very happy. I was able to send home almost all the $84 a week I earned. I didn't need too many clothes and I never went out. But after I got my work permit renewed, my boss changed toward me. He started to make a lot of comments about my being here alone. He used to joke with me that he did not believe my husband existed. And then one night after we closed the restaurant, he offered me a glass of wine. One thing started after another, and he ended up raping me. He told me that if I said anything about it he would tell Immigration and they would send me home. After the first time, it happened every night.

When it was time again for my visa to be renewed, Immigration said no that I must go home. I telephoned my husband. He said no. I must stay in Canada because he was out of work again and the children would have no food. He said I should stay and keep working for a while, at least. My boss said I couldn't keep working at the restaurant any longer. He didn't want anyone without the proper papers, he said. So I took a job as a housekeeper for an Argentinian I had met at the restaurant. I don't like it very much. I get only $30 a week. Of course, I have my own room and television, but I have to do all his washing and ironing and cooking and cleaning and other things, too, for him.

I called my husband again and said I was coming home. It is not possible any more to earn money here. He was shouting at me on the phone saying I could not come home yet. I could not come home yet. But I have decided. I will go. In eight months my life has changed completely. It doesn't matter any more what is waiting for me when I reach my home.

Angela, housekeeper

4   Helge:
Building the country

A grey Victoria winter day. Outside a soft rain falls. The tall, elegant man wipes tears away as he speaks. "Don't know why I'm crying telling you all this," he says with a smile. But there are more smiles than tears in our conversation. "I'll be 70 years old next birthday and I still don't have the sickness that's going to kill me," he tells me proudly.

I had a brother in Alberta in the Peace River country. He was a carpenter who had come here when I was just one year old. I didn't know him. As usual at Christmas you send a Christmas card, but that one Christmas I wrote, "Send me a ticket and I'll come visit you." Lo and behold, there was a ticket in the mail and I had to come.

It was very exciting for me. I came by boat. London-Halifax. Then I got a ticket on a train. You buy a lunch to last you the whole way to Edmonton. I don't remember now how long it took. I imagine it took four or five days, maybe even more by train. It was 1928. Most of the people on the train were immigrants. There were only five Swedish men – boys – that came. The rest were immigrants from Poland, Europe, all over.

The very first experience I had was peanut butter in the lunch kit. Everything smelt peanut butter. I'd never seen it before, or tasted it either. That darn train from Halifax! The smell of peanut butter and the train whistle. I heard that train whistle for years after. The country looked very different, of course. There were big stretches with no people on it. And all the way along the trip people used to buy bread. All the immigrants would run out and buy bread. No matter if they had money or no. There was always someone selling bread.

I got to Edmonton, Alberta and there I asked the conductor about the place where my brother lived. It was called Spirit River, in the northern country in Alberta. I didn't know a word of English, of course, but I managed to explain Spirit River. He just said one word, "Monday." That's all he said. I thought he meant "in the morning." It's almost the same thing in Swedish. But the trains don't go every morning, they only go twice a week. I thought I'd spend the night at the station. But pretty soon, all the lights go out. It was getting late at night. Finally they shut the gate, so I had to jump the fence to get out of the station. I started wandering around the street. I thought I'd just pass the time until morning. Then pretty soon the lights go out all over. The hotels are shutting down. It's 12 o'clock. But I was lucky. I got a hotel where the man spoke Swedish. This was Friday. I got on the train Monday morning.

Spirit River is about 500 miles north of Edmonton. It took about two more days to get there. When I arrived and got out on the station, there was a man. I don't know how he could see I was a Swedish fellow, but he came up and said, "Are you Svensk?" I said "yes" and that I was looking for my brother Ed Holmberg. "Oh, he just went on the train," he said. "He's going to work in another district. Wait, I'll go get him for you," he said. So he went and got him and we met for the first time right there on the platform of the Spirit River station.

I had sent him a telegram but it didn't get there till the next day. Anyway, after the usual things he asked if I'd had anything to eat. He took me to the hotel and asked what kind of meat I wanted. Well, in Swedish there is only pork or beef. So I said "pork." "Bacon?" he asked me. But I didn't even know what it was. We had our meal and then we walked home to his place. On the way there was a pool hall. "Do you shoot pool?" he wanted to know. I'd never seen the game before. So we had a game of pool. He showed me how it works. Then, by and by, we came to his house. His wife was washing clothes. So there I was with my Canadian family. Everything was so new and different, though our conditions there were about the same as in Sweden so there didn't seem to be any real change.

My brother was a carpenter. "How much money have you got?" he asked me. I told him about $20. I thought it was a lot of money. "Oh," he said "you're broke. We'll go down and buy you a pair of overalls." So he paid for overalls and a cap and a jacket, and I went to work with him. At that time they were building a new house in the next town, Roycroft. People were friendly but they took Swedish people like a joke, more or less. I guess they'd reckon we were cheerful or something. They'd say, "Oh, you're a Swede, eh? Oh . . . ." I think maybe it was because we used to drink a lot – whisky and all that. Though I never drank much. I was a bit on the religious side when I came. Never smoked to this day and very little alcohol. But I had a good time.

My brother tried to teach me to read. It's a big problem if you can't say anything to anyone. I liked to read – newspapers, books, anything I could get my hands onto – even if I didn't understand it. I especially liked the comics in the paper.

It was real pioneering up there. You could get these homesteads for $10. I got a homestead up there. You'd just take an axe and go and start to make a field. You'd have to clear 30 acres with a two-bitted axe and burn the brush behind you. You'd cut till one side of the axe was done, then you'd turn it over and use the other. There were deep roots to dig out; then you'd put in a crop. There was wheat and alfalfa. But a lot of years there was a frost and you didn't get anything. The wheat would freeze. But I wasn't dependent on the farm. Taxes were low, about $30, maybe not even that much a year. But you'd have a chance to work it off in the municipality – making bridges and stuff like that. Then you'd build a house. I did that homesteading work in the wintertime. In the summer we were out on the carpentry work.

In that country it gets very cold. Sixty below. I lived all alone. By that time I had a tractor. But I was about nine or ten miles away from the town of Spirit River. The nearest neighbour was a mile or two away. But you didn't get too lonely. You had lots to do cutting down trees. And you had to do your own cooking. Rolled oats and canned milk – Pacific evaporated milk. In them days there was no restriction about shooting animals – deer, moose – there was plenty of those. Whenever you'd run out of meat you'd just open the window and shoot into the clearing outside. We had a trap and trapped bear.

There was never any talk of going back to Sweden. I saved enough money. Could have bought my own ticket. But I had somehow decided to stay. My brother played violin. He was a very good violin player. So he said, "You might as well take up an instrument too and play something." I had previously played guitar, so they said, "How about the banjo? That's good and loud." So I borrowed a banjo and got started on it. We used to play for dances, every week and more. It was a good life. We used to get 25 cents a night for playing. For the carpentry work the first summer we got 40 cents an hour. All those days were 10-hour days. Six days a week. After a while we got 50 cents an hour. Then it stayed like that for a long time because the Depression came on.

I stayed there through the Depression, then I got married. Her parents were Yugoslavian. We built a house for them. That's how I met her for the first time in '28. We didn't get married till '34. I wrote a lot of letters to her. We had quite a correspondence. They must have been good. She understood them. My English wasn't too good but I had a dictionary and I used to look up words. My wife's mother put on a big wedding and they took up a collection. They collected about $13. That was pretty good money.

Me and my brother had bought a workshop where we made doors and windows and furniture. There was a little office in the shop and I made that into a room and we stayed there for a year. I bought a bed at the hotel for 50 cents. A big double iron bed. In the meantime, I built us a house. It wasn't very big, only 20 by 20 feet. One bedroom. Later on, I built another bedroom onto it. In them days you paid about $40 for a building lot. I could only pay about

31

$10 a year for our lot. My wife was a farm girl. She found enough to do fixing up the house. She had always worked hard. Her parents had had a hard time on the farm and she had to help. She never slept on a proper bed until we were married.

I was happy. I used to write home to Sweden a lot and tell them what a wonderful country it was. We would have been really hard up in the beginning, because we had to buy everything, but I had done some carpentry work for a storekeeper. He wasn't able to pay so I used to take out my wages in groceries. That came in very handy when we were married. I had a credit of about $200 or something like that, in groceries. We always had lots of work and were busy and always seemed to have enough money. It was a farming community. The farmers around here had prize-winning wheat.

I was working for a school division, building schools up there. I stayed there for 19 years in Spirit River. We had a family, a son and a daughter. It was a good place for the children to grow up. They had lots of activities — skiing, sleighing. There were lots of things to do in the winter. There was a lot of snow. You should have seen our houses. How poorly built they were! No insulation, no bathrooms. You'd have an outhouse and you'd be sitting there, the snow blowing through you between the boards. There was no water. They couldn't get any water. They couldn't get any water pressure in the dams or anything. There was a man coming around delivering you water. You'd buy water by the pailfuls. We'd have a barrel by the door. He'd come in and slosh the water in the barrel. You'd pay 50 cents to get the barrel filled up.

When we left Spirit River we didn't go very far. We went about 80 miles to a place called Beaver Lodge. By this time I was playing in a brass band. I had a big tuba. They heard about me there in the next town and they wanted me to come down and play in their band. They promised me lots of work there. We played at dances, weddings. I'd sing at funerals. We sold our house at Spirit River. Got about $1600 for it. And then we rented a place at Beaver Lodge. There was all kinds of work. It was easy to settle. There were all mixed people – a lot of Ukrainians up there. But I hated the country by the time I left. There weren't many services up there. Even now, there would be few services there in the Peace River country. There just aren't enough people. I finally came to Victoria where my brother had retired. We lived with him for a couple of years while I built my house. I love it here. Victoria has been good to me.

Now I'm kind of semi-retired. I still work but I don't charge much for my work. It would be hard to stop work. Unbearable, I think, to have nothing to do. Now I just do what I want. I was building an addition to my home, but it got too darned cold for me so I just left it until spring.

You know, I tried so darned hard in the first years to be English. Now I think I really missed something there. You should try to be what you are. It's something you just gradually realize. I never taught my children to speak Swedish. I'm sorry about that now. Maybe it wouldn't have done them any good, but it wouldn't have done them any harm either.

Everybody was hard up when I came here. We were all immigrants. Everybody was struggling. Nobody was well off. It was very hard on the womenfolk. They'd go out in the fields to work and help with the clearing. Then they were faced with having to make meals and put something on the table for the kids to eat. It was rough. Sometimes there just wasn't anything. I know the lady lived on the next farm from me, she finally died of starvation. It was lonely. If you had time to sit down and think you would have been lonely. But I was so darn busy. I just didn't have time. It all just grows on you. I remember the very first time I went back to Sweden. We were all singing, and somebody started to sing "Home on the Range." I started to cry. I was homesick for Canada. It's people like me have helped to build this country.

Helge, carpenter

5 Carmen: You are different

Carmen is within a few days of giving birth to her third child. Only two weeks ago she stopped work as a keypunch operator in a government office. She will go back to her job when the baby is a few weeks old. She talks rapidly. Her dark eyes are quick and bright; her face, cautious and alert. It has been painful to come to terms with her own strength. But now, she will never let it go.

In the afternoon, her two children come home from school. To their mother they speak in Spanish. Together, they quickly lapse into English. She is affectionate with them. However, despite all their pleas, the television remains off.

I first set foot in Canada on December 24, 1966. I came with my infant sons aged two and one. It was one of the most important steps I had ever taken. My husband had arrived nine months before with the understanding that if he found it possible to build a new life here he would send for us. Eventually, he sent the money back for us to make the trip.

It was a very cold, snowy day when we landed at the Montreal airport. A white Christmas Eve. And what a celebration awaited us. As we drove to Toronto my husband told me that he was living with a woman he had met here and he wanted us all to live together. All I could do was cry. I spent my first night in Canada alone in bed with my arms around my suitcase sobbing my heart out. I was just like a child. Nothing in my background had prepared me for this.

I had grown up like any number of Spanish girls. Born into a society full of stupid social conventions, I found as I grew older that people were accustomed to judge things by their outward appearance. I grew up knowing nothing of life or sex. Spanish parents think that their daughters must be kept quite ignorant for the man who will finally marry them.

When I was 20 I met my first husband. We were very much alike, both of us completely inexperienced and timid. He was an only child whose mother doted on him. We started to go out together and there were no problems until his mother became ill. Doctors diagnosed her as being extremely aggressive and destructive. They admitted her to a mental hospital. Now in place of the affection and love she had always shown her son, she began to act as if she hated him.

He was so used to being taken care of that he had no resources to draw on now that he was by himself. With my family he found a real home and a safe place to be. He asked me several times to marry him but, even then, I knew that we were both too young and inexperienced for marriage. The very idea of it scared me. He kept telling me how much he needed to be loved and how even his own mother had stopped loving him. It was a simple way to seduce a silly young girl and little by little I succumbed, believing that with my love he would be comforted and feel less alone.

When I realized that I was expecting a baby, I thought of killing myself. I was terrified of what my family and friends would say. I had always been taught that it was the most shameful thing that could happen to a girl. I knew that at home, once the family knew, they would force me to get married and give me a good beating into the bargain. There seemed only one other solution: to arrange the wedding before anyone found out.

The day of the wedding was one of the saddest in my life. I felt asphyxiated in that white dress. I wanted so desperately to talk to someone who might understand me. But my shame was so great that I couldn't begin to discuss it. Looking at the happy faces of my mother, my brother and all my friends, I felt the most despicable creature in all the world. It seemed I was tricking them all. But at least I avoided the beating and the gossip.

After the wedding we lived in my mother's house with the rest of the family. We continued to be "the children" and never had a chance to find out what it was to be responsible for ourselves. Our son was born and 12 months later his brother. The grandparents took care of the babies as if they were their own, and I must admit that for all of us it was a very convenient situation. We lived like this for three years until my husband decided with two friends from work to come to Canada. When he told me about it I thought it was a good idea. I knew that sooner or later we had to get away from our families and make our own life with our children. I even hoped it might bring us closer together.

Now I was here in Canada and my husband was insisting we live in a *ménage à trois*. He was no better equipped to deal with the situation than I. The only person in any way capable of coping was the other woman. She was from England, older than I and much more experienced. It didn't seem like a difficult, or even an unusual situation for her. I had no idea where to turn. They had taken away my passport and all my papers when I first arrived. I knew nobody in Toronto and there was no telephone in the house. For the first few days I lived like a captive with the two of them. I spoke no English at all but one day when they were out, I went with a dictionary in my hand to a neighbour's house and said the one word I had found, "Telephone." I looked in the telephone book for the Spanish consulate or a Spanish restaurant or somewhere they might speak Spanish. Finally, I found the number of the consulate and phoned and told them what had happened.

A man from the consulate came to see me at the house. He advised me to try to get help to see if we could salvage our marriage. It was arranged that I would have counselling through the Catholic Family Services. My husband came with me. But it was a very difficult situation. He had a job with the government as a draftsman. He had settled into Canadian life very easily. The years he had spent in Spain working for the United States on one of their big air bases outside Madrid had taught him not only the English language but a whole new set of values as well. He was intelligent and ambitious and wanted to better himself. He acted so strangely with me and the children that at times I thought he was drugged. He would scream and shout, then suddenly change and say that he really loved us all. The other woman left the house and moved into a flat a couple of doors away. I knew he was with her every night because he would come home very late only to sleep.

When I look back now I understand it all a little more. I believe he was ill. He was completely egocentric and hysterical. The woman I find a bit harder to understand, even now. In the few days we were all together in the house she treated me like a child. She was very patronizing and acted as if she expected us to be friends. I suppose I acted like a child, too, but I felt so confused and trapped. One day she made a banana cake with icing and brought it to me as a present. She said she knew we would be real friends one day. I took the cake and dumped it on her head!

My husband was very angry with me and said I was acting like someone completely lacking in education. Finally he told me bluntly that he could not live without her and that everything in the house reminded him of her. If I would not leave and go back to Spain with the children, he would make life very difficult for me. And he did. He acted like a madman. He cut off the heat and gave us only $7 for food for a month. Finally, when the baby was ill with bronchitis, I had to accept that it was impossible to share a life with him. We could not come to any kind of mutual agreement. I was advised to leave him alone for the time being. He left the house to go his own way. I went to Family Court to sign desertion papers. It was my chance to make something of my own life, for myself and the children.

I had to decide whether to stay here in Canada or go back to Spain. I knew that if I went back to my family they would protect me, help me, do everything for me and that I would be in the same position I was in before I left. With my family I had always felt like a prisoner. There was no freedom for anything. I felt strongly that

37

as a person I had rights and that here I had a chance to reclaim them. I knew that if I went back to Spain I would lose this chance.

So I stayed. I didn't speak any English. I had two children under three and two suitcases. I wanted to study and learn and do something meaningful and positive with my life. But how? There were a lot of problems to solve. Day care for the children was one of the biggest. Subsidized day care centres were only for children of two years and older. My youngest was only a year and a half, so for six months I couldn't go to school and I couldn't work. I got very little financial help from my husband – only $43 a week. Out of this I had to pay for a flat, for food and anything else we needed.

It was very hard to find a place to live. No one wanted to rent to me because they didn't want the children. Finally we found a place. We had to pay $90 a month, which was a lot for us, but it was the cheapest I could find where they would take us all. The woman who owned the house said on the phone that there would be no problem with the children. She was delighted to have them and would stay with them whenever it was necessary. She was a psychologist. It seemed as if a large part of our problems had been solved. However, after being in the house only three or four days I realized that this psychologist was sexually disturbed. One day after coming home from shopping, I found her completely nude in my bed. She begged me to make love to her. I was terrified and started to cry and scream. I had never seen another woman completely nude before . . . and I felt she was mad . . . absolutely mad.

I had paid a month's rent and so I had to stay there. But I locked myself and the children in my room and avoided all contact with her. I was very frightened. We stayed there for the month, by which time I had found another place. My life at this stage had a nightmare quality about it.

I realized that I had to learn English and applied for the government-sponsored classes where you are paid while you are studying. It was my only hope. I went to Manpower and was dealt with by one of those older women you often strike in government offices, the kind that seems to take a dislike to you on the first visit and then always rejects you however many times you go back. She said, "No. There is no chance. In no way do you qualify." I tried to reason with her telling her that I was responsible financially for my children. She suggested that I ask for welfare. I didn't want to be a parasite. I wanted to do something for myself, to study, to have a chance. How was I going to prepare myself to get a job if I didn't learn English? And how was I going to be able to support my children without a job? I tried hard to convince her. But she just kept saying the same thing, "You don't qualify for the classes. Go to Welfare." I remember feeling very limited as a human being.

Finally, when the baby was two years old, I was able to get both children into a day care centre. But I had no extra money for bus tickets to get them there. I thought that if I found a job cleaning in somebody's house while the children were in the nursery it would bring us in a bit more money. But where would it get us? I wouldn't be learning anything.

I compromised and found a job cleaning two days a week. The rest of the time I went to English classes at the International Institute. When I told a counsellor there that I had not qualified for the government-sponsored English course, she couldn't understand it. They made enquiries for me. I thought it was useless after all the attempts I had made. But they were successful. I was given the classes, which meant that I could study every day from 8:30 a.m. to 2 p.m. and be paid $65 a week while I studied.

By a strange coincidence, the very day that I was advised that I had qualified for the Manpower English classes, my husband left Canada. He just disappeared. If they hadn't given me the classes this time I would have been forced to go on welfare. There would have been no other way.

Now I started a new life. I had to get up at 7 in the morning to feed and dress the children and take them to the nursery. From there I went directly to the school. I studied hard. As soon as I learned English I wanted to take a commercial course to prepare me for some job. But first I had to pass all the exams. I would pick the children up from the nursery, take them home, get dinner, do whatever housework was necessary, put them to bed and then study. I couldn't permit myself the luxury of getting sick. Who would take care of the children? I developed some nervous problems and even had to go to a psychiatrist. He gave me electro-shock treatments for my depression. And I went on.

There was nothing in my life at this time but school, taking care of the children and the flat. I had some friends at the school, other immigrants like myself. A few of them were alone with children, too. Sometimes they would come over to my flat and we would do our homework together, then share a cup of coffee.

I was very lonely. I missed my family and felt homesick for my own country. In my spare time I would write to them all and send them tapes of myself and the children. Then I would listen to the tapes they would send us. I had never been by myself and it was hard for me to get used to it. I had photos of the family and postcards of Spain all over the place.

Life didn't change too much when I started to work. In the beginning I earned only $65 a week. Out of this I had to pay rent of $100 monthly and take care of the children. I don't know how I would have managed if my family had not sent me shoes and clothing for the children from Spain. I put my name down for an apartment with Ontario Housing. We waited just over a year but finally got an apartment in a public housing building. We lived there two years. Two years of fights and drunks, of being afraid at nights, of always having the police around with their sirens blaring. I didn't dare let the children go downstairs alone.

Again, I toyed with the idea of going back to Spain. So far, I had managed to cope with my personal problems, but if I returned it would be to the same kind of life as before. And that was impossible now because I had become independent. I wanted to work and take care of my children and make my own decisions. Still, the idea grew and grew in me to go back. It became a kind of obsession. Go back to Spain and leave Canada. Go back to Spain and leave Canada. And that's how it was until I met the man who is now my husband. Then things started to change.

He is Spanish, too, and works as an air express dispatcher for a large company in the city. When I first met him, through mutual friends, I was still angry and hurt from my first marriage. He had been here a couple of years longer than I and would come and be with the children while I studied. His loving gentleness with the children and his caring for us all made a big difference to our lives from that time on. For a long time it seemed impossible for us to think of getting married because of the problems of religion and divorce. But finally, we realized there was no justification in our not being together and happy and building a real family. When we got married we left Ontario Housing, found another apartment and started to live a more normal life.

The vision of Canada that you get when you are studying English full-time is not very realistic. In the classes you are taught to love the country. It is as simple as that. And it works. You end up becoming very emotional when you sing "O Canada." The teachers are trained to be with immigrants. They are sympathetic, always ready to listen to your problems and to help if they can. But the moment you leave the school and get involved in Canadian life, things change. The people you bump into at your work place or your neighbours at home aren't as tolerant as your English teachers were. They very often discriminate against you, simply because of the colour of your skin or because they don't like your accent. So it takes you back a bit. You realize that this isn't the multicultural Canada you were taught about.

When I finished the commercial course I found a job in the civil service. And I have worked there for five years now. The work is secure and I am now earning nearly $165 a week, but it is a very boring job. You don't learn anything. You don't think. You don't even improve your English. All you do is punch in first names, surnames, addresses. Very few Canadians do this work. They find it unrewarding. And I suppose this, plus the fact that you don't really need much English to do it, makes it a natural for immigrants. There are a lot of immigrant women in my office who finished the same course I did and who, like me, work as keypunch operators.

This creates its own problems. At coffee breaks or lunchtime in the cafeteria, the immigrants always group together. We make friends among ourselves with the English we have all learned at English classes. There might be a Chinese, a Korean, a Pole, a Yugoslav, a Japanese, a Spaniard – but you seldom see even one Canadian. They sit together in another group apart. They keep quite separate from us. This hurts, and we are inclined to feel resentful. The immigrant from northern Europe seems to have it easier. Perhaps it is because physically she looks more like a Canadian, whereas immigrants from the south of Europe, from the Caribbean, from Asia or Latin America often look very different.

The children have never had these kinds of problems. They learned English in the day care centre where there were children of all social classes, of all colours. They do well in school and have a lot of friends. However, life for a child in a family of immigrants is quite a bit more difficult than for a Canadian child. The immigrant child must cope with the fact that at home his parents speak to him in one way and teach him certain things, while at school he learns something that is often quite different. The children resent this. They are young and don't want to be different. They don't even like their friends to know that their parents are Spanish, because in fights or disagreements it is often used to insult them.

One day my younger son came to me very upset, saying that the child downstairs had called him *chili con carne*. Another time, some school friends had come to the house to play and a little later I found one of my sons in tears, "Mama, my friends don't like to come to our house. They say it smells horrible. Horrible Spanish smells." These are just small human cruelties, I know. But they isolate you, they keep reminding you that you are different.

Carmen, keypunch operator

6 Sven and Annie: They promised us gold

It is all very formal in the beginning. Sven in his correct blue suit nervously pulling on his pipe. Annie looking anxious in an attractive pant-suit, her hair curled. And me, trying to make my impersonal hotel room into a warm, inviting place. They are careful about what they say. They want to give me the whole, true story and it is hard to remember some of the details. But as we get to know each other, we all relax. We start to laugh, and the whole story comes tumbling out.

SVEN: What was the beginning of the whole thing? I believe the war had something to do with it. All the schools in Norway were occupied by the Germans. There were a lot of people that had to catch up with their education and of course they picked only the very best. I was not among them. It was 1957. I was 30 years of age. We had been married for seven years and had two boys. I had a feeling I was stagnating. I thought maybe there was a better place somewhere else. I was right.

I had in mind either New Zealand, South Africa or Canada. But then it happened that there was a big double-page centre advertisement in the paper saying to come here to Canada. We went to a meeting they had in one of the big hotels. They promised us . . . actually they lied . . . they promised us gold.

ANNIE: They said that if you were a tradesman it was very easy to get a job. Sven was an electrician. They said he didn't have to worry at all. He had been an electrician for 13 years then. We had to sell everything to go to another country. I didn't like it whatsoever. I didn't want to leave Norway. Sven was the one who really wanted to leave. And I couldn't speak a word of English.

43

SVEN: I spoke five words. To come here, it was a lot of papers to get. You had to get them from the health authorities, from the army you had to have a clearance, from the police to say you'd never had anything to do with them. And all this had to be sent out. Then it came back. We had to go to Oslo to the Canadian Embassy and we had to take the two boys to see them, to see that they were normal. We sold everything – our home and furniture. We had enough for our passage plus seven or eight hundred dollars to bring with us. There were a lot of Norwegians coming here in those years. Especially in '57. I think it was because of the Suez Crisis. We were scared about another war. I used that as a lever to get Annie talked into it.

We didn't know anything about Canada much. The only place we had heard about was Kitimat. We heard about it through some papers that were sent from there to Norway. It said that there was a lot of industry up there. But they told me that the boom was over in Kitimat and it was no place to go with a family. So I said, "Where do I go then?" They told me Victoria was a nice place, very much like Norway. So finally I said I would go to Victoria. *(Sven is quiet for a bit, drawing on his pipe. When he starts to talk again his voice is tight and dry.)* It was a terrible thing to leave home. It was really hard. You had to shut off all emotions then.

ANNIE: We took a ship from Bergen. Everybody came down to the dock. It was just as if you were going to die. The boys were three-and-a-half and six. They didn't really know what was going on. They were standing there waving to their grandmother and grandfather and aunts and uncles and cousins. And everybody was crying . . . and then we were just leaving and. . . .

On the boat we met another Norwegian couple. And they had two kids. They were going to Victoria, too. We never saw them before. But that really helped us. We got to be the best of friends, just like a family.

SVEN: We came to Montreal. Then we just went directly onto the train within a few hours. This was something we really hadn't bargained for. Because we had the two small boys we bought more expensive accommodation on the train. A small compartment. We had the brochures and they showed us how it would be. We came on the train and they packed us all into this coach where people were sleeping even in the middle of the floor.

ANNIE: We couldn't explain anything. We didn't speak English. We just had to take what they gave us. At night, at 8 o'clock, they hoisted these beds and then the porter came through and swept off the dust and a cloud of dust settled on everything. You didn't know who was sleeping above you or below you. Before we got off the train we were sick as dogs – throwing up. It was from excitement, from the dirt, the food. Four days on the train was a lot when you're not used to it. The food didn't agree with us.

SVEN: And the country was different. We'd never seen prairies. It was so flat. . . . I remember we had a big trunk of books – very heavy. And these had to come on the train from Montreal. Now everything was included in the ticket to Victoria – all our household things we had brought with us, but they said the books were not household items. And I had to pay $22 to have this trunk of books shipped from Montreal to Victoria. $22. It was a lot of money to us then.

There was no ferry to Victoria in those days. There was just a ship would go Victoria – Vancouver – Seattle, in a triangle like that. It left at 10 o'clock at night if I remember right and you arrived there at 7 o'clock in the morning. When we came ashore here we didn't know which way to go. They had told us in Oslo at the embassy that when you arrive at your destination the officials from Immigration here will come and meet you and help you to get settled. There was nobody there of course.

The other Norwegian we met on the ship he knew a bit more English than I did. He phoned down to Immigration and spoke to them. They said, "We haven't got anything. There's nobody here."

Then they hung up. It was a Sunday morning, and it was the day before Victoria Day. We started walking around to find a hotel. There was no place. While we walked from one place to the other, the wife and the other one and the kids were sitting outside the post office with the suitcases. It was a very beautiful day. Nice and warm.

ANNIE: We had quite a bit of luggage with us when we were sitting there, and people who were walking by were looking at us funny.

SVEN: The other man and I were walking, trying to find a place to stay. We came down Johnson Street to a hotel that was there. It had a long staircase going up and outside the band from the Salvation Army was playing. We came up to the first landing and one of the officers in the band came after us and started talking. As it came out later this hotel was a place for prostitutes and he thought we were customers and he came after us to try to save our souls!

We got the message across to him. "Wait until we're finished playing," he said. "We'll see what we can do." So he got in touch with one of his superiors and they found a room for us. We came into the New England Hotel here – an old, old thing. Cockroaches and everything. It was terrible. But it was a place to stay and there was nowhere else. Everything was full up. The Salvation asked us what kind of church we belonged to. And they got in touch with the Lutherans here. The Lutheran church happened to have a member that was a Norwegian and he come to the hotel.

This man from the church turned out to be quite a prominent man in Victoria. He had been the conductor of the symphony here. He was quite a musician and he was also operating a little carpentry joint on the side. A factory. He gave me a job there to start. Just a temporary one. They drove us around and showed us everything. They were so good to us. I remember I was out walking the day that he came. Yeah, I was walking. I couldn't take a bus because I didn't know where they were going. And so I walked and walked. And my feet were just like – with big blisters all over them. According to what the officials had told me, I was going to have no trouble. But unemployment was very high.

ANNIE: When this man came to the hotel and knocked on the door, I didn't know who it could be. I didn't know if I should open the door or no. I couldn't speak the language, and there were so many drunks. So I didn't want to answer the door. But this man said, in Norwegian, "I can speak Norwegian. I've come here to help you." Oh, it was such a good feeling. They helped us find a little suite. A very nice thing it was up by the water.

The other family who was with us, after a couple of days when he could find no work, they went back to Vancouver. Said it was a bigger city. We didn't hear from them for a couple of weeks. But then she wrote me and said it was terrible over there. I phoned her and said they should come back here and stay with us. I thought that maybe we could all rent a house together. So that's what they did and eight of us stayed together in a one-bedroom flat. But you know, it was all right. At least we were together and by then we all felt like a family. Then we rented a house and we had the upstairs and they were downstairs.

SVEN: He eventually got a job but I couldn't find anything as an electrician. I was being angry. I went to the Electrical Union, but they just shrugged their shoulders. At that time I worked for a building company building a school. I was carrying planks for the carpenters and earning $1.50 a hour. I remember that first time we went out shopping. We went to the nearest grocery store. We didn't have a car or anything. It was so much. We had two big shopping bags each. And it only came to $10. We'd brought a little money with us, too, so we were able to buy beds and a bit of furniture. We weren't too bad off really.

ANNIE: One thing we never knew was that here you could buy old used furniture. We had no idea about that. You don't have those second-hand stores in Norway. So we bought new furniture. If somebody had told us it could have helped a lot then to buy second-hand things.

SVEN: It was a whole new world. What I remember most of Victoria in those first weeks was the different smell in the stores. I suppose it was the different kinds of vegetables. I remember that very well. The whole world smelt different.

ANNIE: The food was *so* different. Even the meat had a different taste. You had to get used to all new things. Another thing I really noticed here (of course it has changed because here is modern now) was that the inside of the stores and houses in Norway was more modern than in Canada. This really surprised us because we had heard a lot about America being so glorious and having everything.

SVEN: Victoria itself was beautiful. People were wonderful. We could go for a walk in the evening past the gardens where people were working and they came out and talked to us. Fantastic people! I remember one night in that first little flat we had, Annie sitting at the kitchen table writing letters home. I guess the tears were dripping down on the paper. There was a woman living in the apartment right beside us and she was walking back and forth. She must have spoken to some friends and told them there was this Norwegian woman living there and crying all the time because they came, these Norwegian people. They had come from the prairies. They came to see us. They were very nice people. That's how we started to know people here. I did go to the YMCA for a few nights. They had some English classes there. But I only stayed a few nights because there were so many different nationalities there and they all spoke their own language. There was no way you could learn anything.

ANNIE: I also went twice, I think, and it was the same with me. It was nice to see all the people but I don't think I could have learned any English. And what they were talking, I already knew that much. Our oldest boy he started school right away in the fall. He was very upset when he first started school here. He was a quiet boy and he wasn't outspoken. He started to stutter. I felt so bad. I used to take him to school and when I got back home I'd find him behind me. He didn't want to go in. So I had to take him back. Then the teacher helped. She was an immigrant too. She'd come with her parents here. So she knew what it was like. She took him after school and gave him extra help. She felt, too, that he was lost. But it was amazing how fast he started to learn then.

SVEN: The niceness of the people here was so tremendous. That helped us quite a bit. Except for the immigration officials. We got absolutely no help from them. After I'd been to the Electrical Union and they wouldn't do anything, I went down to Immigration. I wanted to hold them to their promise of a lot of work. It was in the days of the Hungarian crisis. There were a lot of people. The whole house was full down there. I told them what I wanted, that I wanted to get into my trade. They asked if I had a job. I said "yes" that I was carrying planks for a carpenter on a construction site. So he told me, "Here we've got the place full of Hungarians who have nothing and you're coming here complaining." I said I wasn't concerned with his problems, that I wanted a job in my trade. It was the first time, the only time, that anyone has ever thrown me out bodily. And they did. Took me by the arm and down the stairs and onto the sidewalk. It was the last time I ever went back there.

ANNIE: I think that after half a year, if we had been able to go back to Norway, we would have then.

SVEN: After half a year . . . well, maybe . . . no, I don't think so. I still had my pride. I wouldn't have gone back then. I got a job after a while with B.C. Forest Products working on the production line. My first job was to clean the boilers in the power house. I had to shovel the ashes out. There is caustic soda in the wood and I got some in my eyes. I had to have three operations on my eyes for the caustic burns. When the accident happened it was a Sunday. There

49

was no first aid man on duty and at first the accident was not reported.

Later on, when I filled out the form for the Workmen's Compensation Board, they didn't accept it. Said it didn't go through the usual routine. I wrote to them to explain. There were two or three letters I got from them, and the last one was to the effect that if they heard any more from me they would take me to court for trying to defraud them. So I didn't do anything more. But B.C. Forest Products they kept me on the payroll. "Walking wounded" they called it. I stayed around there and did odd things like sorting papers and I still got my pay. After about 14 months on the production line, there came an opening in the electrical department and that's when I got a job again in my trade. My salary jumped then up to $2.64 an hour. That made a big difference to us.

ANNIE: But there *were* some hard times. What about when you were on the production line and there was a strike? He wasn't getting any money at all. We had just bought an old little house. We even had to borrow $200 of the $500 for the down-payment. Something had to be done, so I got a job in a motel as a chambermaid. I couldn't really speak the language, but I could work. I worked full-time and earned 85 cents an hour. At least we could pay our bills. I kept on working for a year and a half. It helped me to learn the language and to meet people. Both the boys were in school. Then I got pregnant. When I was six months pregnant, I quit.

When I remember back I think that all the difficulties we had in those first years kept us all closer together. And when Sven had only $1.50 an hour and we had to be careful with money, I think we had the best time of our lives.

SVEN: I'm still with the same company working. I been there for 19 years now. They been good to me. But I been pretty good myself. The job I'm holding now, I never could hold in Norway. There, they're very strict with diplomas and things. If I was going to hold a job like this in Norway, I'd have to have engineer's papers. Which I don't need here. That's the good thing about it here. When I was first getting the job I had some papers – trade papers and the like – and they said to me, "We're not interested in papers. We're interested in your work. You show us what you can do. If you can do it, fine. If you can't, you're out." I think that's a very good way to do it. At least, it helped me.

But I still think that the Canadian officials in Norway, either they didn't know or they didn't care. They did say though, I remember, they said, "We are not really interested in you. You are not ever going to become Canadian. It is your children that are going to be the Canadians." Which might be right, but I feel as much Canadian as anyone around here. We found a new country and we really like it now.

Sven, electrician, and Annie, housewife

II

WORK
IS OUR
LANGUAGE

7 Starting all over again

You have to get a job. That's the first step always. But where do you start?
Everything here seems to function without any need of you. You must create
your own place. Convince people they need your skills, your strength. It's a
whole new beginning. It isn't easy. It's even harder than you thought it would
be.

The machinery is the same

The system of mining here is very different to what I used to do in
Chile, but there is something common to all mining work everywhere. The machinery you use is the same. It doesn't really make
any difference what language you speak. Although, to the immigrant it makes a difference. Because of your language, or your lack
of it, you are treated with a certain amount of suspicion. So you
work hard. You work hard to prove yourself, to show that you are
worthwhile, that you know what you are doing. It's important to a
person. To an immigrant, work becomes his language. The best
language he can use.

Victor, miner

A proper job

In Kenya, they told me that my qualifications as an electrical engineer might not be recognized here and that I might have to sit
exams. But I still decided to come. As Asians we felt very insecure
because of the political climate there. After the Ugandan experience we felt it was time to leave. People there are afraid. Within
East Africa, Uganda was the most stable country and we thought

that if something happened like that, Uganda would be the last place. It was the first. Then it started in Ethiopia, in Zambia. People try to make the most of life down there but they feel insecure. We were working for our living. We are not wealthy. I was born and brought up in Kenya and so was my father before me. But suddenly these things start happening. I had two choices – Australia or Canada. So I came to Canada.

From Nairobi the first point I arrived in Canada was Vancouver. I stayed there about two months and got a job as a TV repairman. I didn't have my license, so I was doing mainly bench work. In Kenya, I had worked as a development engineer for the government broadcasting organization, but fortunately my hobby had been repairing TV sets. It came in handy in Vancouver. I was earning just enough money to get by and, of course, I was making applications all over the place for a proper job.

I applied to CN. I sat for tests and all. They took me on and sent me to Edmonton for three months training. The standard here is not what I expected. I am a graduate in electrical engineering and at the moment I'm a telecommunications technician. My ultimate aim is to get a job as an engineer. To sit for the professional exams. I applied to get my qualifications assessed, and they said I've got to sit two exams. I'm young and I guess I expected to have to start at the beginning. It's hard though when you have to start all over again.

Shirish, telecommunications technician

Agriculture

I had done my university training in Switzerland where I had studied bacteriology and microbiology. On the ship they asked what my qualifications were. When I told them, they wanted to know if I was interested in agriculture. I said "Yes." So they sent me to a tobacco farm near London, Ontario. I had to pick tobacco.

Klara, immigrant counsellor

Bluffing

I went to the Manpower office as I had been told but there were no jobs for me. For two months I went, and at the end of that time, there was still nothing. I was feeling completely demoralized. I went again to Manpower and explained to the counsellor that I was nearing the end of my money. He told me to come back the next day. I did so and the next morning he handed me a cheque for $150. This was to tide me over. I was furious. I threw the cheque back at him and told him I had not come to Canada expecting charity. I was strong and willing to work. I would work at anything.

He seemed quite taken aback and finally suggested I go to work in the garment industry. I was quite prepared to do this, but I didn't even know how to thread a machine. I asked if he didn't have something that I might know a bit about. He said they would have to check into it. I left the office and went home. I was very depressed.

Then my friend said she knew of a job in the payroll department of the company where she was working. However, she advised me not to put my full education qualifications on the application. "Instead of your degree, just put one year university," she advised me. It was the first time in my life I had lied but I was desperate. I went for the interview and they asked if I knew how to use the computer. I said I thought so. Did I know how to make up a payslip? Well, I had done basic mathematics, I explained, and I would learn quickly enough to do it the Canadian way. I bluffed my way through the interview and was told to start the next morning.

I was very nervous. I had to start working out the payslips. I had no idea what to do. Fortunately, there was a very nice English girl in the office and when the manager left I asked her quite frankly to show me what I was supposed to do. For 30 minutes she sat down and carefully went over the whole thing with me. It wasn't difficult and when the manager came back it was all done correctly. What a relief it was. And from there on, I had no trouble at all.

Linda, social worker

Shoe shine

For me, it's never been too hard. Just the usual. You come and you gotta find a place to work and a place to live. And maybe you gotta find some people. Friends, you know what I mean? But just the usual. For me, it wasn't bad. I'm single when I come. And in Montreal, this fella in Immigration, he says to me that if I go to Alberta it's better for me. Plenty of work in Alberta, he says. You gotta go to the West and straightaway you find plenty of work. I get the train and I come to Alberta. I go first to Calgary, but there's nothing there. At Manpower they say that in Lethbridge they got plenty of work. I go to Lethbridge, but there's nothing.

One day I'm having a couple of beers and I meet this fella. He's another immigrant come from Yugoslavia. He's a fella not speak too much English either. Just like me. But he tells me about a job picking the sugar beet. It's not bad, he says. So I go picking the sugar beet. I do that for five weeks. It's pretty hard work. One day this fella says he's driving to Calgary. I go with him. All my life I live in a big city. To work hard that's okay. I wanna work hard, make a bit of money, make a new life. But I don't like to work on the farm.

When I come back to Calgary, they tell me again the same story in Manpower. Not yet. No jobs. So I walk around the streets. Then I say to myself, why not do what I did in my own country? In Italy I used to clean shoes. A shoe shine. People they need their shoes cleaned even in a big, rich country. So I find a place where they got a barber shop. "Hey," I say to the fella. "You need somebody here to clean shoes. A man comes in and gets a shave, cuts his hair, gets the shoe shine." This fella, the barber, he laughs at me. But I don't let him stop with the laughing. You got an empty stomach, you got a full head pretty fast. Full of ideas. So I keep talking. I tell him the possibilities. For him, it's good. He pays nothing. All he puts is a bit of space. I do the whole thing. So I tell him the next day I'll come back and start. He laughs at me and shakes his head. "Crazy Italian," he thinks. But I know. I know what I'm doing.

I got just a few dollars. I go buy some brushes, polish, get some cloths. Next morning, I come back to the shop. Still, he's laughing. But he gives me the space. Just a chair I use. Just like a regular chair. A fella comes in and he has his hair cut. I start to talk to him. Don't ask me how because I speak no English. But I start to talk and pretty soon I'm cleaning his shoes. They like it. I make not too much in the beginning. Sometimes I don't even charge. Just to show them. But after a while they start to like it and I do a good job. So I stay there.

The barber, he likes it. "It's good for business," he tells me. And he's right. I make a living and I'm happy. I'm not gonna be no millionaire. But I make a few bucks, save a few bucks and after a while I get married to a nice girl. No problems. We got two kids now and it's pretty good the life here. Steady, always steady. Once in a while when I need a bit more money, I start to help a fella down here. He's building kitchens in the new houses. Some nights and weekends I go with him to earn a few bucks.

It's not too difficult to make a living here. The secret is you get the life in your hands and you grab it very tight and you don't let it go. But some people, they don't got the strength inside to hold on. Maybe the life is too much all the time for them. Too much for one pair of hands. I know many immigrants, just can't take it. Good people, willing to work hard, but they just can't take it.

The life for an immigrant is hard. Very hard. Lonely. Very lonely. Especially you come to a city like Calgary. You no have friends. You no have family. You know nobody. That's very hard. All the time for the newcomer it's making the new life. In the old life in America, the immigrant come and break the new ground. Maybe they come on the horses and fight bang-bang with the Indians. It's hard for them. They gotta break the new ground. But I tell you something. Today, it's just the same thing. It's still the new ground you gotta break. Only one difference. Now, the Indians they come to the city just like the immigrant. And they gotta break the new ground, too. Just like the immigrant, the Indian in this country. The life is hard. Very hard. You just gotta hold on.

Enzo, shoe shine

8 We're used to working hard

You are prepared for the first difficult period of adjustment. You knew before you came you might have to work at any kind of job just to get on your feet. You're a worker. You've always worked hard. But you have dignity, too. You're a worker – a man, a woman, not just a cog in somebody's money-making machine.

Sewing sweaters

I got work in a factory where they make sweaters. I sew up the shoulders, the sleeves, the sides. It is very dirty work. If I work all day on white sweaters, I am covered in white dust and fluff. Then I have to spend time before I come home getting cleaned up. Some of the women get rashes on their faces or their hands from the chemicals in the fibres. It's tiring, too, you know, when you sit all day from 7:30 to 4:30 with just a half-hour break for lunch and two 10-minute coffee breaks. It is especially hard now that I am pregnant again. But I need the money and I'll probably do the same as I did when I had the last baby. I worked about two weeks longer than I had to and I started earlier back to work, too.

When you're there, there is no way you can stop for even a minute. If you go to the washroom you have to go fast, or else the foreman comes to look for you. If he finds you talking, you're fired. It's a big factory and there are about 200 of us, almost all immigrant women. We get $2.80 an hour, so it's not too bad. It's a job. It's funny though. I spend all this time on a machine and yet I can't sew. I don't understand the machine my mother owns.

Maria, finisher in sweater factory

Sticking together

We were always caught in the middle out here between the Ukrainians and the English. I worked for a while in Winnipeg, then I moved on to Moose Jaw and Lethbridge for a while. It was always doin' the job you could get to do. Whatever was goin', we'd be the first to go do it. We worked like blazes – Italian, Portuguese, sometimes a Greek fella or two, and a few others, Germans, whatever. We were all kinds strapped together by the bloody hard work, the filthy conditions in the camps or wherever we had to live, and by the pidgin English we spoke.

We had fun though. There was more spirit in the pack of us than I've seen now for a good 18 years. The songs we'd get going between us. Even the jokes! I'm damned now if I know how the hell we could tell jokes with no one language between the lot of us but, by God, some of the best jokes I ever heard in my life I heard in those years. We worked at railroadin', clearin', construction. One winter we worked in Saskatoon buildin' the airport. You'd work a while then there'd be a lay-off. You'd never earn much – $1, $1.25 an hour maybe. But you were here and there wasn't nothin' else to do.

They weren't bad days, y'know. It's like the war. After you live through the bloody horror and the hard times you look back and all you can think about is the good times. The jokes, the songs, the way the guys stuck together. You were brothers out here in those days. The guys were really loyal to each other. I think we thought we'd better stick together so they wouldn't get us. Not the Ukrainians, not the English. We were "wops" or "dagos," DPs or what the hell, speakin' our own language – de-cap-i-tat-ed English, I'd call it. Maybe de-val-u-aṭ-ed English would be better for it. We weren't Ukrainian and we weren't English. And I tell you somethin'. It's still the same out here today. There are them two camps hold the balance of power and the rest of us is just caught in between.

Gino, construction worker

61

White threads

I've been everything – domestic, cashier, salesgirl, dishwasher, waitress, factory-worker – and the factory business was the worst. When I went to get a job this personnel manager says to me, "You ought to be doing something else. You won't like factory work." So he gives me this big nail – like this, about five inches long. And I have to go up and down these blue jackets and take out all the white threads. All day, hour after hour, doing the same thing. Taking out all the threads. Your eyes give way after a while. Your head aches. And after two weeks you see white threads everywhere. You get on a bus and find yourself reaching out to pluck threads from some man's jacket. I tell you, you start to go mad. And the women in the factory are popping aspirins here, tranquillizers there. It destroys you.

But you've got to be strong to allow yourself to be destroyed. You know what I mean? Most women won't allow themselves to succumb and go under for a bit knowing they'll come out in the end. You keep thinking, "I got my kids and who'll take care of them if I succumb." But one woman I know had the courage to go under for a while. She's got six kids and now she's all right, and she's got them all back with her. That takes guts, let me tell you. I never had that much courage. I fought it all the way and it was hell. I tell you it was hell. I had to place the children in an institution for two and a half years.

I finally got a job as a counsellor for immigrants. After I was working for about eight months and things were a bit stabilized, I got the children back home. It hasn't been easy. But we all try. We try to compromise and to understand each other. They have missed and I have missed. But I have done my best.

Irene, counsellor

Dirty business

I never, not in Holland or anywhere, saw such a dirty, stinking business as there was on that farm in Linwood. After we came by boat to Halifax we got a train to Guelph. When we arrived at the station in Guelph it was 6 o'clock in the morning. The farm owner wasn't there to meet us. You see, there were two stations there and he went to the one. He didn't think we might be at the other one. When we weren't there, he just took off again and let us sit. We were all tired and dirty-black from the soot of the train. It was a train they were using for immigrants. On the whole wagon there was only one faucet to wash ourselves.

Anyway, there we were with our 10 children waiting for three hours and a half. We could hardly speak English. But we had been told we would be picked up, so we just kept sitting there. It was 9:30 when he did come to pick us up. He took us to the house but it was still occupied. A family was still living there. He was the biggest, laziest bum I ever have seen. He was still milking the cows at 11:30 in the morning. He didn't get out of the house until that night and it was about 11 o'clock before we could put the kids to bed.

At 6 o'clock the next morning I had to start milking the cows. I didn't know anything. There was no one to tell me where to find anything. I found the milking machine under a pile of manure. I tell you, when I seen that – boy, it was the only half-year of my life I will never forget. This was a kind of situation I never even would have believed would exist. There was never somebody from the government immigration department to see what was going on. I never saw anyone. They didn't care.

Albert, retired

Rash

It was when the skin started to come off the fingers of my left hand that I went to the doctor. They did a lot of tests and said it was from a chemical we used in the plastics factory where I worked. It was like a rash that spread all over my arm. But I'll go back to the job when I'm better. That's if I can get my job back. I haven't worked now for four months.

Aspasia, worker in plastics factory

Assembly plant

I don't know if you can have six or seven nervous breakdowns one after the other and still keep going. But I'm sure that is what happened to me. I lived for two years without smiling even once. I didn't cry either, but I never smiled or laughed. One day, my little girl said to me, "Mama, why don't you ever laugh any more? Why aren't you happy?" That did it. I started to cry and I couldn't stop. I cried for four or five days. The doctor gave me shock treatments and after that put me on tranquillizers. But it didn't really help. I only lost two weeks at work because we so badly needed the money, and I couldn't afford to lose my job.

It was a terrible period. I would feel sick each morning going in the gates of the plant and up the stairs. I used to sit there seeing those little round pieces coming up and down in front of me. I'd think I was the only person in the whole world. Shows you the state I was in. There was a whole row of people sitting either side of me and across from me. But they were all locked inside themselves. We didn't look at each other or talk or smile. We had a half hour for lunch, and even then we didn't talk much.

I would think of myself as I had been when I was a little girl at school. It didn't seem possible I was spending my life like that. It is all over now, of course. And I didn't lose my job. But something inside me has died, I think. Maybe something dies inside us all.

Sandra, assembler in small appliance plant

64

Bronchitis

I am used to working hard. I worked with my husband on the farm in the Azores and there was always something to do. But when he died, life there was impossible. There was not much for men to do and it was even worse for women. My two brothers were already in Canada, so I came, too, with my 12-year-old daughter. I was 59 years of age. We came to Wheatley, Ontario and lived with my brother.

I spoke no English, but it was not hard to get a job. I arrived in August and I spoke to some Portuguese people and they spoke to someone they knew. In September I started work in a fish factory. For three years and two months I worked there. It was hard work – nine hours daily with a half-hour for lunch. I would start work at 4:30 in the afternoon and it was usually 2 in the morning before I got home. I earned $82 a week.

There was so much fish in that place – very cold frozen fish that would freeze your hands. I worked on an assembly line and the fish would go by so quickly that you would have to work fast to keep up. And then there was a lot of water around, too. Hot water. It made the whole place hot and wet and steamy. I had to wear boots because the ground was so wet, and we were given plastic aprons and head coverings.

It was a very big factory and there were lots of immigrants working there. The foreman was Portuguese, but the bosses were Canadian. We were often laid off when work was slow and then I would go to a farm to pick vegetables. But for the main part of three years and two months, I worked in the fish factory.

The factory was beside the lake and it used to get bitterly cold in winter. One day, after I'd been working on the assembly line, the boss took me off it to work on a machine preparing onions. This machine was between two open doorways, one of them looking onto the lake. It was the middle of winter and I had just spent hours working on the assembly line and was all hot and sweaty. I stood

65

there in this cold draught and caught a very bad cold. It seemed to get lodged in my chest. I felt I couldn't breathe. It may seem foolish to say it, but that day changed my life.

I got very bad bronchitis. I was sent to the hospital and was there for two hours but they did nothing for me. I was out of work for several weeks and when I applied for compensation I was given $80. Then after a few weeks, they gave me a paper to take to my boss. But the boss spoke only English and I don't speak any English. And anyway, I couldn't walk to the factory. I could hardly breathe and there was no bus or no one to drive me from the town. So I never went back there. I never took the paper to the boss.

After a while I spent three weeks working in a wood factory. But I couldn't breathe with all the dust there and finally I had to stop. Then I got work as a cutter in a garment factory. But again, the dust from the fabric irritated my chest and my throat and I couldn't stay.

I live now in Toronto with my daughter. I don't work anymore. I would like to. We need the money. But my daughter is married and at least I am able to look after my little granddaughter while her mother is working. I still find it hard to breathe. The doctor gives me medicine. But it doesn't seem to help. It makes me angry. Everything was fine for us while I could work. I got sick at that factory, my health is ruined and compensation did not help me at all. They just gave me $80. But what can I do?

But with all the problems I have had here, I like Canada. I like it very much. There is a future here that we never knew in the Azores.

Isabel, housewife

9   If you can find a job

Sometimes there is little chance to prove yourself. You try to reason that your past life must count for something. Your work experience. Your education. You feel obliterated as a person. But jobs are not easy to find, and without a job there is no way to take root in this new land.

Any kind of work

Life is hard here, but if you can find a job, it's all right. There are no jobs in my country. It is as simple as that. We came here from Haiti about four years ago. I do not want to talk about that. We had a cousin here and we came, my wife and I, as visitors. We got jobs. She was a sewing machine operator and I worked in a factory where they made small electrical parts. She earned $1.70. I got five cents more. We could live but only just. But we were lucky. We got landed in the amnesty the government granted to immigrants in 1973. Then our children were born. Now we have two. One nearly two years old, the other only three months.

There is no work and yet you must put food on the table, put a roof on your head and clothes on your body. My wife has had no work for seven months. I had a job with the city last summer cutting grass in city parks. Now I'm on unemployment. I get $75 dollars a week. It's not enough money to live. We want work. Any kind of work. I can get that job back with the city in April, but I must find something until then.

We don't have many friends. It is so cold here that you don't go out. You go to your job if you are lucky enough to have one. Then

67

you go home again. There's no time for much else, anyway. When my wife worked we left our one child in a house where a woman took care of three children. You must do that if you have to work. But just two weeks ago, here in Montreal, a little two-year-old Haitian girl was beaten to death by the husband of the woman who took care of her. He was Canadian. The little girl was annoying him, he said. That does not make us feel good. This is what it means to be an immigrant.

Hubert, unemployed

Just one chance

There have been adjustments to make and it has cost our family much heartache and many headaches. It is hard for the children. They already have to cope with the problems of growing up and then suddenly it is twice as hard. Because you are growing up different. For my husband it has been very difficult. He is a man with a lot of pride. Not too much, but just a proud man. He is a good man. He is concerned about his family. But he came here and has had very bad luck with jobs. "Do you have Canadian experience?" "Have you done this work before in Canada?" How can you ever do any work in Canada unless someone gives you a chance to start? To start somewhere, that's the only chance we asked for.

When it was difficult to find work he would be cross with the children, even with me. I tried to understand the changes in him. I knew he was worried. But one night I couldn't stand it any more and I started to scream at him, to scream and to hit him. And you know what he did? He cried. My husband cried like a child.

It is not easy. We miss our families and wonder often if we did the right thing coming to Canada. But you have very few choices. There was no work in Ecuador, no future for the children. We had to come.

Angelina, domestic

Filled two hours ago

I did economics at university but I can't get a job in my own area of occupation. I don't like doing what I'm doing – but the fact that I'm black contributes 99 per cent to my being unemployed.

We are not given the opportunity to improve or to demonstrate what we can do. I was in Ottawa in May and I applied for many different jobs. I have my honours in economics. All of my class-mates are working. They started to work right from school. They all got jobs. There are jobs. Many times, I'd phone companies and they couldn't distinguish who you were. They'd say, "Come on right away and apply for the job." You'd go and they'd see you were black and they'd say it was filled two hours before. That hap-pened many times.

Charles, unemployed

Too old for this country

I came here two years ago from Warsaw. I came because my daugh-ter is here and I wanted to be close to her. I hadn't seen my daughter for many years and it was exciting when I arrived and saw her. But I am not happy here. All my life I have been a working woman, a productive person. I worked 35 years as supervisor of the accounting department of a very big company making medical instruments and supplies. But I am too old for this country. I know that now. This is a land for young people. Life for them is good. I did not realize this before I came. I knew I must learn the language, but I thought that I would be here close to my daughter and that life would be much the same as before.

My life now is nothing like my life before. I live alone, I go to classes and do what I can to improve my English. But the days are very long. I read, I go to concerts, I shop, but I feel unproductive in this society. I am just an old woman who cannot find a job because she speaks such poor English. But what can I do? Life goes on. I cannot go back. I gave up my apartment there and my job. At my age it would be hard to start all over again even back in my own country. So I work at my English. I keep hoping that once I learn the language it will be better for me here. But the language is very hard. Sometimes I just cry because it seems I will never get it into my head.

I am very lonely. I feel that if I could get a job it would be easier for me. I am prepared to do any kind of work. I don't have to be boss. I just want to do something. But it seems impossible. I have learned that old people should stay in their own countries where they know people and are known.

Ludwiga, unemployed

10 A way to make things better

When you are just one more cog in the machine there is little you can do to change the way things work. But once you get together with all the other cogs, you suddenly have a lot more clout.

Organizing

What I want more than anything else is a little peace. For nine months now there has been nothing but trouble and it has been hard on my health. I couldn't sleep or eat. I was depressed and nervous. I have grown old in the past nine months. It was not good for my husband and my two sons who live at home, either. One of my sons is now in high school and the other works for a lawyer at city hall. My two older boys are married.

It all started in June last year. I was cleaning at the Ontario Government offices. I worked from 5:30 in the afternoon to 10:30 at night. I earned $2.40 an hour. We worked hard but the money wasn't very good and some of us were not satisfied, especially when we knew that at Queen's Park office cleaners were being paid $3.40 an hour. A dollar an hour more than us.

So a few of us decided to try to get a union in our company. But one of the supervisors heard about it and I was told that if there was any more talk of union I would be fired as a trouble-maker. I didn't want any trouble so I decided to let the matter drop. And a little bit later I went to Portugal for a holiday. But when I came back, the women were still unhappy with the pay and the working conditions. We used to get only three paid holidays a year – Christmas,

71

New Year and Good Friday. And we were not even paid regularly. Sometimes it was nearly three weeks between pay cheques instead of two, and that was especially hard on the women who were without men and who had to support their children.

In February, we decided to try again for a union. I collected signatures of the workers plus a dollar from each one. It wasn't easy. Many of them were afraid and would say, "I don't want any trouble. At least I've got a job. If there is trouble what will happen to my children?" But we tried to make them understand that a union could help us. I used to stand outside the building to get them as they came out of work. And in February, that's cold work.

Then on February 19, when I was cleaning on the fifth floor where I always worked, the forelady came to me and told me, "You better get out of here fast. Get your things and get out of the building. You can't work here any more." She told me it had something to do with the signatures I'd been collecting for the union.

I was scared but I knew I hadn't done anything wrong. I had the signatures in my bag and at first I hid them. I stuffed them in my dress. But then I thought, "No. Why should I have to hide anything?" And I took them out and put them back in my bag. I went down to the basement to the manager's office and asked him why I had to leave. He called me a trouble-maker and told me to get out and go home. But first he wanted to know what I had done with all the signatures. In the beginning I lied to him. I told him I had thrown them out. He said that I could have my job back only if I promised not to try anything more with the union. But I argued with him and told him I had not done anything wrong. I worked hard and had been there for three years – longer than anyone else. Finally, he told me to get my things and go.

I was very angry. I knew it was unjust. So as I was leaving I told him that I hadn't thrown the signatures out at all, that they were all safe in my bag. I went home and told my husband about it and he said I was right in what I had done. But I couldn't sleep. I'd never had any trouble like this and I didn't want any.

At 11:30 that night the phone rang. It was the forelady. She was in tears and said that she would lose her job too if I didn't hand over the signatures. "Please," she said, "please let me come and pick them up." I spoke to my husband and he said, "Let her come." So at midnight, she arrived with the manager's brother, who said I was giving them all a hard time, that his brother was very young, and so on. The forelady was desperate. "At least you have your own home and your family to take care of you. If I lose my job, it is different."

They promised me my job back the next day if I gave them the signatures. So I took the four pages of names, addresses and phone numbers and in front of the two of them, I tore them up into a million pieces. The manager's brother didn't want them torn up. He scooped up the pieces and put them in his pocket. As they went to the car I heard them say, "There is no way she can ever come back to work for us. She has stolen money from the company." I knew then that they had tricked me.

That was Wednesday night. By Friday, eight women including two foreladies were out. I found later that while those two were at my house, the others at work were all herded into one area of the building and the area was barricaded with tables so they couldn't get out. Just like in a jail. Then they were all forced to sign a paper saying they did not want a union. When some of them refused to sign they were told to go. The others were frightened and they signed. Then they were told from now on they would be able to take a 15-minute coffee break, something we had never had. They were all issued with uniforms too, that night.

The eight of us who were fired took our case to the Ontario Department of Labour and they helped us a lot. It didn't matter that we couldn't speak good English because they had a translator who was Portuguese. She told me the company would have to pay me for the time I was out of work. It was 80 hours.

We had to go to a court where there were representatives of the company and three judges. At first, they wanted to pay us only 50 per cent of the wages owing to us, then when we refused they said 75 per cent. But we still would not agree and finally, after many phone calls to the head office of the company in Montreal, they had to agree to pay us the full amount. We were told we could go back to our same jobs. We didn't really want to, but we knew that if we didn't we might lose everything.

Already we were feeling a bit stronger and by April, we had a union. Conditions were going to be better – $2.90 an hour, 12 paid holidays a year instead of three, and lots of other benefits. Then in September, we were all told that the company's contract had expired with the government. Another company was coming in that would pay less money and we were all out of a job. For most of us, this was serious. We don't speak good English and cleaning is the only kind of work we can really do. But now we felt strong. We fought it through with the company and the government.

At first the new company said, "We do not want these women; they are trouble-makers." And the government man said, "I have no power to stop the contract." But we told him, "You have power for everything." Now we all have our jobs again and they say our pay will go up to $3 in January.

I'm tired now and I hope it will be better and peaceful. I am in Canada for 10 years. My husband was here 12 years before that. I have been working at my job for three years and this is my very first job working outside my home. We don't want any more trouble.

Leopoldina, office cleaner

Tired of fighting

I am tired of fighting. When we first came here we were strong and full of hope. We knew it would be hard. We didn't believe stories of the streets paved with gold. But we did believe in other things like democracy and having as much chance as the next person.

My husband got a job quickly. He is a good carpenter and some-one he knew gave him a chance. We worked hard on our English.

We went to classes at night and would try to read the newspapers.

After eight months my husband was laid off his job. "Maybe in six more weeks," they told him. "There is no work right now." There was no work for my husband for six months. After the first few weeks he started to get very depressed. But fortunately, I found this job in a factory making stockings. After having had a job where all I did was clean some other woman's house, a job in a factory made me feel I was doing something important. I was happy to be out of the house with other women, too.

It was hard work. Not heavy, but tiring. After a few hours sewing the same little strip, my eyes would see two, then three, then four stockings in front of me. All at the same time. At work there was no time to talk. It was all piece work so it was important to keep working. I used to sit there and go off in a dream and my body would just go on doing the same thing, the same thing. Sometimes I used to think I was a machine working a machine. And I used to wonder who was working me.

Even though it was tiring, our conditions were better than in some of the factories because we had a union. It had just started when I began to work there. It meant that we had eight paid legal holidays every year, and they had even won some increase in the piece-work rate. I became active in the union because it seemed the best way to make things better.

After 14 months there things started to go bad. Work slowed down. Workers were gradually laid off. I lasted a few weeks because I worked hard. It was important for me to keep that job. My husband was working on and off, but he had not been working steady. Things between us were bad, too. There was always so much tension and many, many problems. I thought that if we could have a bit of money, something a bit more regular, it might help us get closer again. But I eventually lost my job, too. A funny thing happened. All of us who were really active in the union were not able to get other jobs in hosiery factories. We never knew why and could only suppose we had been, how do you say, blacklisted.

That was two years ago, and I have had 10 jobs since. Somehow we get by each month. There is just enough to pay for rent and food. But I wonder now if it will really get better? Maybe we were wrong in the beginning and this is the only way it can be.

Marie, office cleaner

Boss

We tried so hard to get a union where I was. And every time things got going, there would be lay-offs. One day, the boss called me into his office. He started out very reasonable. I was stupid. I thought he really wanted to talk to me. It was the first time he had ever spoken to me. I started to tell him how we felt about organizing. How I felt it could improve the way the women felt about their jobs. Suddenly he changed and he stood up and yelled that if I didn't watch out he had fifty lawyers that could get me out of the country in a week.

Tessie, factory worker

Bloody limey

I had been a trade unionist since I was 14. When I arrived here I was anxious to do things the right way. I went to Manpower. I was told I'd have to get a license. Where do you get a license? City Hall. I went to City Hall and made enquiries there. They didn't give you much information. "You've got to sit a test," they said. "Fill out this form and it'll cost you $5."

Next thing I found out the trade union organization that took care of plumbers. I went up to the union. A guy came and asked, "What can I do for you?" I told him I'd like to join the plumbers' union. "You would, would you?" he said. "You're one of those bloody limeys." I could have socked him right there. "I'm not any bloody limey," I told him. "I happen to be a Scotsman." "Is there a difference?" he asked. Then he adds, "You've got to be a fully qual-ified apprentice, you know." I told him I'd served seven years as an apprentice. I put my hand in my pocket and took out my credentials plus my London and City Guild Sanitary Inspector Certificate. So he says, "Those papers are no bloody good to me. You can take them to the washroom with you." I got so damn mad I said, "Look Mike, you can take your union and shove it. The next time the union is mentioned, you'll come to me. I won't come to you." I slammed the door and walked out.

Naturally, I had to take a non-union job. Three years later, this non-union shop where I was working started to build up, and Local 46 felt they had to organize a shop. They swallowed their tonsils and they came to me to see if we could organize one. It turned out just exactly as I thought it would.

Jim, plumber

You've got five minutes

When I got to Sudbury I didn't know a soul there. I'd just been advised by a bank manager in Midland that there was lots of work there. I started to enquire around and learned that the biggest job was in Copper Cliff in the International Nickel plant. Bryce Fraser was the man to ask for. I took the streetcar over there and went in to the plant. I asked the gate-keeper, "Where's Bryce Fraser's office?" "It's in the plant," he said. "You can't get in there. You'll just have to wait till they come up." Then I asked him how I'd know who was who when they came up. "I don't know," he said, "That's your headache."

So he shut the gate at the punch alleys, where you punched as you went in. There was a timekeeper at each alley. A sort of keyboard. I looked the whole thing over carefully. The next morning I put an empty lunch box under my arm and I got one of the cards and I punched it. Of course, the guy didn't suffer no hardship because his card was punched when he came in. I got in and went to Bryce Fraser's office, got hired and got my tools. Several of my friends that were left back in Midland, I wired them and told them to come up right away. They used the same trick and got in and got hired, too.

But a few months after that the crash came. There were no fewer than 5,000 men standing every day at the gates to the plant looking for work. They were all immigrants. Most of them were Slavs or southern Europeans. It didn't take you long to find out that time-keepers and sub-foremen would give some poor devil a job if he had enough money to buy a job from them. He'd get in and go to work for one or two pays, then they'd fire him and somebody else bought the job. But that was only for the mine company. I didn't see that taking place on the construction job.

People thought it was a temporary lay-off. The steelworkers, the plasterers and brickworkers, they were all organized people, but the carpenters weren't. We started to organize the carpenters' union. Of course, we got fired as soon as we started. The company had its spies and everything was leaked. I remember once after we got the union, the Finns on a construction job were on a strike. The men went out and scabs were brought in by the company. The Finnish women – wives of the strikers – got pretty fed up with the fact that their men were out and these other fellas had been brought in. So they got together, pretended they were meeting for coffee, and worked out a plan of action. They marched up to the site and told those scabs, "You've got five minutes to get out of here. If you're not gone then, we'll strip you naked and run you through the streets." Those fellas moved out as fast as you could think.

When the war broke out, things began to look a little better. Then after the war it didn't take long before it started with the little recessions. That went on every year for a while. Immigrants continued to come up here after the war, but they were mostly southern Europeans. A lot of Italians, a few Spaniards and Portuguese. And Finns. There were a lot of Finns. There was an enormous increase in the union movement here in the first three or four years after the war, so gradually all the jobs were unionized. Conditions for immigrants really improved then.

Eli, retired

11 Making something of your life

You come with so many dreams. Then as time goes by the dreams change. They fade. You learn to find contentment in reality. But sometimes, just sometimes, the dreams really do come true.

From a patch of nothing

We are survivors of the Second World War. We were victims of the Nazi terror. We spent time in jails and concentration camps. So when we came here we were humble because of that. The purchasing power of the dollar and the amounts that you can make fascinated us, of course, but it didn't make us wild.

I was already 45 when I came so that made it difficult. But I managed. I'm a graduate accountant but because of the lack of English I had to work as a labourer. I didn't speak a word of English when I came. I worked first in greenhouses as I have a heavy background in horticulture. For 17 years I was an accountant in the Department of Agriculture in Yugoslavia.

Of course I went to English class when I came. I worked very hard. I went to professional courses, too, other than the straight language classes. I had to learn a technical English. I felt frustrated, of course, that I couldn't just go on with my profession when I came here. But that is the problem of all professional immigrants. You have to rewrite exams, re-do diplomas. But I was prepared for this before I came. I was ready. I considered this as a sacrifice, as a price I had to pay to emigrate. Finally, after I passed all sorts of exams at all levels, including a special five-year course in advanced accountancy, I had the qualifications that I needed. I became the equivalent of a chartered accountant and for 14 years I was the chief accountant of a steel company in Kingston.

Now, I'm retired. I do a little work still – a little bookkeeping on the side, a little translation. But my needs are very limited. I have my four beautiful grandchildren, and I've built a garden there out the back from a patch of nothing. I did not ask too much of Canada, but I have worked hard and have managed to make something of my life here.

Fred, retired accountant

Up to the individual

I was working on the green-chain gang at this lumber mill just outside Prince George. It was a fairly substantial mill, one of the biggest ones in this area, but due to poor management it went into receivership. This helped me to get the exposure I needed to advance. It was circumstantial, but I got exposure to the appointee of the bank. He told me, "I'm going to keep an eye on you." And that's what I needed. Two weeks later I was a green-chain foreman. Wherever I was working I always set myself the next step up. Not too high, but a bit farther than I could comfortably reach. I needed motion. So when I was made green-chain foreman, I knew I was being noticed.

I had plenty of problems there. There were a lot of guys pulling on the green-chain and then suddenly I'm made foreman. I was a bit of a fanatic. I did a good job, a better job than most other people, because it was the only way I could get spotted. For instance, I was there 15 minutes before we started to get everything ready so that at eight o'clock I could start. Most people resist that. But I had to make my stand. I insisted that the job be done and done properly. I told them before noon that if they weren't prepared to do it the right way there would be another five guys there to do the job at one o'clock. At one, I had another five guys lined up and I said to the first five, "Okay. What about it?" "No way," they told me. "Fine," I said. "You're fired." They all left. At 4:30 they were waiting for me outside the gate. I was scared, but I knew I had to face it. I said to them, "Do what you want. I'm right here. I'm not tough. I'll see you all in court." They thought it over and it just kind of washed out. That was all over and done with.

I was promoted to mill foreman, then yard foreman. The mill kept deteriorating. I kept getting promoted because people were axed down. I was promoted a lot faster than I could keep up with. Then the receiver came in and chopped most of the management off and before I knew it, I was in the number three spot in the company. It had taken me a year and a half.

I wanted to get my own mill. There was a mill came up in Watson Lake in the Yukon Territory where they wanted a general manager. I had an option on 40 per cent of the shares of the company. It was a small mill, only about 13 men. A real challenge. I was a good operator but I ran into problems with about seven of the shareholders. My idea was to build a company. Theirs was to soak as much out of the thing as they could. They were just about broke when they brought me in and capital was hard to borrow. I didn't know their motivations. I thought they might have been looking for a tax write-off, which meant I would be the manager of a company that went bankrupt. I didn't like that a bit. I didn't want it in my references. I knew that one way or the other I had to leave.

In the meantime, I had acquired half-interest in a motel up there. It was a buyer's market. The people wanted badly to sell. They were desperate to get out. I came in the back door, more or less. With a $5,000 loan I went in. I felt the Yukon was going to grow and Watson Lake was the central point, the hub. I was too eager, I guess. I thought this was something that was gonna work. I left the lumber company and started to run the motel to try to make a go of it. I thought I'd get it going and then we'd sell it and I could get back to the lumber business in the central interior.

Being ambitious by nature, I got into the thing and started pounding nails here and pounding nails there, expanding the place. That was a rough period for us. We were there four years. We couldn't get out. I'm a lumber man and a social drinker. I had to be there in the bar every night – waiter, bartender, bouncer. And there were some dandy ones there. Those guys come out of the bush and they're ready to start roaring. I had guys pulling knives and all, up there. I'm lucky I'm still alive – no bent nose, no teeth missing. It was a struggle all the way. No matter how much you worked at it, there was only so much you could take out. It was impossible to get help. One summer, I fired everyone in the kitchen and all summer long I had to do all the cooking myself. I'm no cook. I can't even boil an egg. But what are you gonna do?

I don't like to give up but it was not a healthy environment. By then I was married and our daughter was born. I decided to leave it and lease it out. I'll never get any money out of it. I've written all that off. But I had to leave. I came back and went into lumber again. Slowly I started to build up myself again. I'm a fairly versatile guy. I've done everything. Now I've started my own mill. I started very marginally. Everyone said it couldn't be done. But we're extremely successful.

What I've been able to achieve here would be impossible in Europe. Here, an individual has a lot more control over his destiny. Regardless of who you are or what your background is, you have complete control over your own future. It's all up to the individual. In Europe it's extremely important who you are, where you were born, what diplomas you have, where your family stands on the social ladder. Here, all that is totally irrelevant.

John, lumber mill owner

Come with a vision

It helps to come here with a vision. We knew what we wanted. We had a goal to work toward. For us, it wasn't that hard. I am coming out of a bakery. My father was a baker too. For about three years I worked in different bakeries here, but our idea was always to start a bakery of our own.

We came with only $300 to our name, the clothes we wore and not much more. And we came with our little daughter. We arrived on Saturday. My wife went to work on the Monday and I started Wednesday. It was very different for me. I was working the night shift and at that time you had to work harder here than in Europe. In Germany in my own bakery I used to work 20 hours a day but here, you had to work faster. The output is much higher here. I earned $70 a week and after that, I worked part time for a dollar an hour. I started working at midnight and worked the next night till 9 o'clock.

We moved into a small suite to save money on rent. There was a garage came with it, so I started building my tables, coolers and everything I would need in our store when we started. I bought out a bakery that went bankrupt – showcase, different machines, breadpans. Then a friend of ours, also a baker, made a rental agreement with the owner of this shopping plaza before it was even built. At that time, they would never have given me a lease because I had no name. I was nobody. So he got a lease and he transferred it to me when we were ready to open up.

My wife and I worked very hard in the beginning. I worked nights and she worked days. I do all the baking myself. There is nothing sold in that bakery that wasn't baked there. Not when we started and not now. I got recipes from friends, and then we tried to adjust European recipes to this climate. We couldn't use our recipes here because of the climate. We couldn't even use Toronto recipes. They won't work. The humidity in the air is much lower here. Things dry out much faster. In Europe we bake bread without adding any shortening but that is because we have different flour and humidity. We didn't need any shortening.

If I look back, I think the hardest adjustment for me was to the food. Nothing tasted the same – the meats, eggs. Eating a hamburger bun or a wiener bun was out of the question. Even today, I cannot eat white bread. I still eat rye. Fifteen years ago, there was no choice of pastries. What did the Canadians know? Cinnamon buns. They didn't even know salt-free butter.

The business didn't go well in the beginning. People came in and said, "There have been other bakeries here that went broke. You're going to go broke, too." It was a rough area to start. There weren't too many houses around here then. The very first year was awful. We had the baby in September, then we bought the store in November and the house, just across the road, in February. It was hard. Sometimes I felt like not waking up in the morning. I'd be working all night and my wife had to start at 5 o'clock. We used to take the phone off the hook in the house and in the shop, so we could hear the baby if he started to cry. And our little girl, she was only four, she had to babysit a lot, too. It was rough on her. It took us about a half a year until we decided if we would go on or if we would quit.

It's a big financial outlay to start but we had friends who helped us out in that. For instance, one friend gave us a load of flour and said whenever we had the money we could pay him for it, even if it took a year. My brother had started his bakery three months earlier and I got some shortening from him. I guess the biggest financial burden was the oven I had to buy. It was $3,000 at that time. Then we had to pay for the house. We had to have the down payment. You had to take the money out of one hole and shove it into another.

It was maybe three years before we felt we could ease off and relax a little. Sometimes you'd have people quitting on you so you'd have to jump in. You can't find a replacement overnight. It is very difficult to find people that are trained. It takes three years apprenticeship to be a baker. But you don't find people easy. Especially now that the government gives them more unemployment money. They can live on unemployment for weeks. So who wants to work? They're brainwashed. We have a just society, so every-

84

body is going to make enough to live on without working. Who wants to work? Just a few stupid ones. We can't complain though about hiring people. Our people are with us for a very long time. One girl is in her eleventh year with us, and then one baker eight years, the other one, six.

One of the bakers I have did his apprenticeship in my shop. Now he's a baker and he never left us. The other was a baker in the old country. We haven't got any training for bakers here. Now they are just starting. Nobody wants to work in a bakery because of the early hours. You must work from 4:30 in the morning during the week, 3 o'clock on Friday, and midnight on Sunday. You work eight hours and you bake then enough for the day. You have to calculate how much you need to bake. It's hard sometimes. One time you run out, another time there is too much. But you make a good living if you don't have too many problems with staff. We're settled now. We're Canadian.

Karl, baker

Clown

I was born in Italy near Mantua in the Po valley in 1938. I later went to England where I met my husband, a Canadian, and I came to Canada with him in 1968. All I knew of Canada was that it was cold. As a matter of fact, when my mother knew I was coming she went to a store and bought me a whole lot of ski suits which, of course, I never wore. I think I ended up giving them to the Salvation Army.

I taught school for several years, and then we went back to England. By that time my husband was a sculptor and went to England to study on a Canada Council grant. I followed him there of course like a good wife. Our son was born there. After that we came back to Vancouver, where I did a number of different jobs before I finally started a circus.

The circus was really a fluke event. We started it as a project – something to do in the house where I lived. At that time there were about seven or eight people living in the house and we thought we would perform as a circus in a fair that was happening locally. By the time we had drunk a lot of retsina one night, we really got going. By the end of the night we had the whole show planned. There was a belly-dancer, a fortune-teller, a strongman – and I was going to be the clown. After the performance people started asking us to perform again. They even offered us money for doing it. It really blew our minds. So, I've been a professional clown ever since.

Being a clown is for me my way of communicating. If you feel while you are on stage that you have that contact with the audience, then you really know it. It's a feeling of being really together. And when you have finished, when your clown turn is over, you are truly elated. It is the most challenging thing I ever have found to do. Being a clown, especially if you don't rely on gags or props, or things like that, is really like putting yourself totally naked in front of an audience with only whatever is inside you and laying it all out. The audience laughs because they see a reflection of themselves in you. So you must be totally open. It doesn't happen all the time. I'm still a very young clown and I guess that being a great clown means being always totally in tune with the audience.

You try to get the audience to feel – to feel emotions, either of sadness or happiness – any feelings at all that there might be inside of you. If you can tell them by your expression or by whatever you are doing so that they can feel it too, that's what being a clown is.

I am a European-style clown. I wear a bowler hat that is really in shreds. My jacket has gone through two and a half years of washing. I burnt it first with bleach, so that every time I wash it now, a piece of the jacket comes off. It's as if my clown history lives through the jacket. The first harlequin, the very first clown, was Grimaldi in the Commedia dell'Arte and his costume was like this. It was only in the 18th century that harlequin became very elegant, his costume coordinated in colour and design. The earliest harlequin jackets were so messed up that they had to have patches all over. That's how my jacket is. My pants have blue and white clouds with red hearts flying out of them. I like to play good emotions with the audience. I like playing with fright and love. Those things that are very Italian. It's very soap opera. I think I am still very much Italian, either I really suffer or I'm off sky-high.

There are very few women clowns in the world. It has been mainly a man's field. I haven't even seen that many good clowns around. American clowns don't usually make me laugh. They are very plastic, very cliché. Charlie Chaplin is my favourite. Buster Keaton I love too. My clown is very asexual. I wear a white face, thin blue eyebrows, I use my own shape mouth painted in coral. I used to wear a red clown's nose but I found that it really bothered me because I play a lot with my eyes and it just got in the way. I felt it was something phony. I didn't feel comfortable with it. I am a silent clown though I do sing, and I play music. I started teaching myself the accordion this year. Skills like that are very much part of a clown.

I went to clown school last spring. A man from Ottawa came over. It was a six-week course. There were about 20 of us taking it. We used to work from 10 o'clock in the morning until about midnight. It was really a process of finding your clown. The clown is really inside you, it's part of you. I already had my clown pretty solid even before this, but the course helped me a great deal. It showed me different kinds of channels and it also showed me the need for skills. I had started with my clown when I didn't even know anything about it. I learned how to improvise with the audience, to take clues from the audience and play on their response. It doesn't matter if they respond with tears or laughter, you learn to play on that.

I love Italy. I like the spirit of the people. But I love Canada too. It took me a while to get used to it. I spent my first year here crying because I wanted to go back to Europe, but when I came to B.C. my life changed. It reminded me of when I had lived in London; there was more of a feeling of neighbourhood. I find that life here is nearer to my own soul. Here I find I have more options about the

87

kind of life I can live. In Italy, I belonged to an upper middle-class family and there were all these "dos" and "don'ts." Here, I do what I want. At the age of 36 I decided to become a clown and I just got on with it.

Ida, clown

A brand new car

I remember once about 20 years ago I got a phone call from somebody in Immigration who told me that there were some people there who had just arrived and who spoke Spanish. They asked me if I would go to visit this family because they were so disappointed with what they had found here. It was a German family who had lived in Spain for many years before the war. I went down to talk to them and they were packing their bags. I asked what they were doing. "We're packing our bags to go back to Germany," they told me. "We have been in this country a week and we cannot stay any longer." "Wait a minute," I told them. "I promise you that you will get a job here and in one year's time you will have a house and a car."

"You're crazy," they told me. "Just wait," I said to them. "What's more, I am going to ask you a favour. After you have been here for a year and you buy that car, I want you to come and take me for a drive all around the town."

They thought I was mad. But they stayed. One day, the following year, there was a knock at my door. When I opened it, it was this family. They used to come often to visit me, but I hadn't been expecting them this day. I asked them to come in.

"We're not coming in, you're coming out," they said. I went out with them and there was a brand new car. So they took me for the ride they had promised me.

Denora, dressmaker

III

A NEW WORLD

12 The powers that be

You've been thrown into a complex, unfamiliar world. There's always someone saying you mustn't do this, you must do that. You have to deal with governments and agencies, with hospitals and schools. But it's hard to know how you should act. Everything you do seems to mark you as different.

Expulsion

There have been many times when I have been sure I was going crazy. And many times when my husband and my children thought it, too. I feel in myself, you know, a kind of dignity. Do you understand me? I feel I am a good person with much to offer, especially to those close to me. But it has been destroying for me in the past five years to see the look in the eyes of people in the street, in stores, in buses, when I have met the teacher of my children at school. It is a cold look which tells me I am different. It supposes I am not so good, not so equal. After a long time of this, there are days when I start inside myself to believe those eyes and what their cold looks say. Then sometimes I start to do crazy things.

One day my boy brought home a piece of paper from school. The words were hard for me to understand. I think also that I become afraid whenever there is a paper from school. I worry it will be something bad and that I will not be able to do anything. I read this paper many times and then I began to understand what it said. I understood it to say that my son was not going to be allowed to stay in the school. That they were throwing him out.

Something inside me broke up. Maybe it was the pain of leaving my parents and our friends in Greece. Maybe it was all the worry about our life here and if it would start to go all right with jobs and a home to live in. Maybe it was all the hope that it was worthwhile what we were doing for our children. I don't know what it was but I went crying like a crazy woman out of the house to the school to tell them not to do it. That my son was a good boy. That he had to go to school and learn many things.

At the school somebody took me to the principal's office. He had no idea what I was saying. Perhaps I was speaking Greek then. I don't remember. I think maybe he was worried I was sick or something had happened to my son. They called my husband at work. He was very worried when he came and then he became very angry. They did not want to throw my son out of the school. The piece of paper said that they were putting him in a higher class.

Dionysia, housewife

Baby

Four years ago when I went into hospital to have my first baby, I was about 27 hours in very difficult labour. They wouldn't let my husband come in to see me and no one in the whole hospital seemed able to speak my language. I was in great pain and was frightened. I couldn't sleep because the pains came all the time. But the baby wouldn't come.

About five different men, all doctors I suppose, came in to examine me. They didn't talk to me and I couldn't say anything to them. I just was there in the bed and they examined me. Then they came for me in a rolling bed and took me to the operating room. I started to scream. I was so afraid. And then I woke up. I felt very sore but the baby had gone. I screamed and screamed and the nurse came and was angry with me. But it was not for two hours more that I knew I had had a Caesarean section and my little girl was brought to me.

I think I suffered some bad shock through this experience. I was unable to talk to anyone and once I had seen my baby I didn't want to see her any more or feed her. They moved me to another part of the hospital and then the psychiatrists came and talked to me. This time there was a woman there who spoke my language so she could tell me what they were saying. But I didn't want to talk to them. They asked many personal questions about my husband and me and what we did when we were in bed. I didn't want to talk to anyone.

I stayed in hospital for two months, then I came home. I want to be with my family now. This is not our country. But my husband says we must stay. He says always that things will get better for us. I am very lonely here, and I do not want any more children.

Lina, packer in biscuit factory

Will you stay forever?

When I was having my first baby I went only twice to the hospital before. I was so scared, because I never spoke any English. Then when it was time for the baby to come I went in with a big suitcase – the one I'd brought from Portugal – and it was all filled. I had everything for the baby. Nobody told me they supply everything in the hospital. The nurse she asked me if I was going to stay forever. Oh, my God, I felt so stupid.

Aida, housewife

Scared

I was scared when I came here. I was only five. I thought it was going to be really ultra-modern like in the books. I thought Canada was part of America and when they talked about America you thought of New York and huge cities. But my dad made a mistake when we were leaving the airport. He took a wrong turn and instead of going to Vancouver, we went all around Richmond. There was this bunch of cows and horses sitting around all over the place. I thought, "Holy crow, we've just retrogressed back into time." I was expecting to see huge buildings, 50 maybe 100 storeys high, and there were only cows and farmhouses.

The only English I knew was one - two - three - four - five - six - seven - eight - nine - ten. When I got to 11, I said "one-one." I got laughed at for that. I was teased an awful lot. I was a bit introverted when I came, scared of the kids. I couldn't understand what they were saying so I just went into books and read and read, I'm still a bookworm.

My first couple of teachers in grades one and two were just awful. I didn't understand much English then and they sometimes had to repeat things because I didn't understand. One of them especially lost his temper with me. I thought it was pretty unfair. It wasn't my fault. I had a lot of trouble in those years. Kids used to tease me a lot, but I beat a couple of them up. They left me alone then. In grade three I still had a lot of problems with grammar, but in grade four I started getting 85 per cent in English. That helped.

Nobby, 14 years old

I got lost

I've been here one year and four months. My first impression of Canada was that it was all white – it was all snowy. It was colder than Jamaica. And I didn't know anyone. I felt good when I was going on the plane and when I was coming to the airport in Canada. I want to be a stewardess like my aunt when I grow up, 'cause I like riding on planes. I wouldn't mind being a pilot but I don't think I'll ever have enough money to buy a plane.

I feel funny when I start school because I don't know anyone. I got lost once and when I went back to school the next day, they started to tease me that I got lost and I didn't know the way. But that was the first time I was here and I went out on my own. That made me feel awful. I don't like when everyone teases me.

The school work here is easier than in Jamaica but the teachers shout at you. They don't do that too much in Jamaica. The kids are different here, too. If you're in a fight and someone beats you and you didn't run they tease you here that you can't do anything, and if they ask you to do something and you say "no" they call you "chicken."

Karin, 11 years old

What can one man do?

LILITH: The baby was born in June and I didn't get a job until September 21. It was at Trans-World Records. They offered me $3 an hour. There isn't much to tell about that job, just that I stayed there one night and I had an accident.

I had been to school during the day and I started work at this new job at 12 midnight. It was a place where they pressed records. And that's exactly what I was doing. I was pressing records. It was a fairly big operation. There were three shifts and about 30 people on each shift. I hadn't much time to see the whole thing but this machine I was working on was a mould. It had this one big thing at the top and another at the bottom, about two and a half feet across. You had to put this liquid stuff in it. Two of us were new – myself and a boy – and this girl was supposed to show us what to do. Well, she showed us and then she said to go and work on this machine. So we were working there. At 4 o'clock, the woman working with us said, "You go and take your break and when you come back, I'll go and take mine." When we came back, the other girl left me and the boy to do our work on the machine and she went on her break.

It's a machine where they have two lights. Whilst you're standing between these two lights, it's not supposed to close. It stays open as long as you are standing between these two beams, as long as the beams don't meet. I was very careful about that. I was just there putting the stuff in the machine and the machine came down on my hands. I was standing there one minute and then I just felt it on my hands.

AUBREY: It was a big steel press. It has a 1,000 pound steel pressure and that would create a closing weight of about five tons. That's the pressure they need to mould the record.

94

LILITH: It was as if I waited there a long, long, long time before any-one actually came to me. Finally, someone came and I took out my hands. My hands were crushed so flat. . . . I don't remember being afraid. I remember . . . the first thing I thought about was. . . .

After the hands came out and I saw them . . . the fingers after they came out they were crushed . . . they extended long . . . they were long and flat . . . they were like this together. The first thing I remember saying to myself was. . . .

One of the girls she came and held me and said, "Go and sit down." But when I looked at her the first thing I said was, "But my hands . . . I can't do anything for my children." That's the first thing that came to me.

I guess there was lots of commotion. Everybody was running to and fro. Some of the people were crying. They called for an ambu-lance then and I went to the hospital.

AUBREY: I was at home. You see, when she got the job we had a problem to get someone to stay with the children immediately, so I decided to stay home that night, to give her a chance to start work.

I got a phone call about 5 o'clock in the morning and was told there had been an accident. The person told me that her hands were crushed . . . badly . . . and she couldn't use them any more. I called a friend to stay with the children and I went to the hospital. When I reached the hospital, I couldn't see the hands because they were all tied up.

LILITH: After I reached the hospital, the only thing I could remem-ber was that this doctor had come to me and said, "What happened to you?" I said, "I don't know." He asked me my name. Well, I didn't tell him immediately. All I could remember was that he was cutting these clothes away. I had on a long-sleeved jersey and it was crushed into the hands. So all I could remember was that doctor cutting, cutting away the clothes. I remember they gave me an injection. I didn't remember anything else.

AUBREY: She wasn't conscious when I saw her that morning. I spoke to the doctor and he said they would have an emergency operation. They said they would try to save the hands. They said it was a 50-50 chance. Lots of things went through my mind. I felt that . . . not from my own part but from her own part . . . that she could become very useless. I know how she feels about her children, caring for them and so on, and without hands she would definitely be sensitive. . . . All of these things started to go through my mind. How, if she was able to endure the pain and remain alive, how could we adjust now to the new situation?

Every day I look back at the whole situation I tend to say that first of all, because of this, we are or we were being harassed by Immigration. They found out everything. Immigration came after us approximately two months after the accident.

LILITH: I spent 52 days in the hospital. I had five operations. They kept trying to save what they could of the hands. Not all of them, but at least the hands and a few fingers. At first I thought it was useless. I saw the state they were in. But then people kept saying to me that they have all this medical know-how and they could do things, miraculous things. At first I thought they would just take them off, but then I started to hope again that they would take off a few fingers only. But every time they would do an operation, they'd take off a piece more.

AUBREY: Your hopes would keep going up and down. The first time the doctor spoke to me, he told me, "Her fingers are badly crushed. But if there are live tissues we might be able to save the hand." After the first operation, he told me he might be able to save the whole of the left hand except for one finger and she would lose about three fingers on the other hand. We were very, very hopeful then. But the week after he told me they'd have to take the hands off because all the tissue was dead.

LILITH: It was hard to take. I kept trying to adjust to what they said. At least, I said to myself, I have some life.

96

AUBREY: All these operations, specialists and everything were part of our problem. You see, at the beginning we were working under assumed names because we didn't want any problem with Immigration. So she was working under a false name. When she went to the hospital she had to give them the false name. They asked for identification and the identification had her name. So this created a problem. We went to a legal aid lawyer. I told him the whole story. He said he was going to look at it. He notified the hospital that the name she was using was an assumed name and he gave them the correct name. He then started to look into the possibility of paying the hospital through the Workmen's Compensation. So they are handling this now. In fact, Workmen's Compensation have now assumed the responsibility.

LILITH: After I had the accident, Aubrey had to stay home for so long with the children that they weren't able to keep the job for him at Plastic Age. We had a few savings so we used that to live on. Then the place where I had the accident, Trans-World, told him they could get a job for him. So I said to him, "Aubrey, you better not accept that job. I couldn't think of your working there." But we needed the money. He asked the lawyer if he could take a job there. At first the lawyer said no, but then he agreed. So on the Monday, he started to work. And on Tuesday, Immigration raided the place and they picked him up.

I have my own ideas about that raid. You know that all the time I was in the hospital, not one executive of that company ever paid me a visit or sent me a message. That company didn't have to pay a cent for what happened. And they knew that the machine that I was working on was defective. The general manager said to a friend that he knew it was defective and they had the part ready to put on it. He said that to a friend and the friend told Aubrey. And when the Workmen's Compensation inspector went into the factory there, he found that the machine was defective and he sealed it off. He found quite a few other defective machines in that factory.

97

AUBREY: There are two agencies working against the company now – Workmen's Compensation and the RCMP. The RCMP are against them for hiring illegal immigrants. They hire a lot of illegal immigrants even without being aware of the fact that they are illegal. Illegal immigrants work hard and they need pay them less. Me, for example. I was not illegal but as a student I was not supposed to work.

However, when I came here I had to go to school. I had to meet my school fees, pay the rent, buy food, and still maintain my children back home. So I always worked. I always worked with the fear of losing my job if I did not work hard enough. So that means I always put in extra hours to impress and in the hopes of getting an increase. You start even going against your conscience. You work overtime voluntarily and you work overtime without pay, just to keep this job. So of course these companies like to hire illegal immigrants. They know they will work very hard – efficiently and without any protection.

The day that Immigration raided Trans-World they got a lot of illegals. I was surprised just how many there were. I was the last person to be interrogated. The officer said, "You're illegal here. If you cooperate with me, I will cooperate with you." I was operating under an assumed name, but I was legal in the country. What's more, the person whose name I was using was a landed immigrant in the country who had left Canada and gone back to Guyana to work. I was using his social insurance card. I showed it to the immigration officer. But he was in doubt. So they arrested me, handcuffed me and took me to RCMP headquarters on Dorchester Street to question me. While we were going there, this immigration officer who seemed sure I was illegal, tried to trick me into admitting it. I couldn't understand why he should just assume I was illegal. But I didn't want him to know my whole story, so on the spot, as he asked me questions, I made up a story of how I had come to this country through Red River from the United States.

When we went down to the RCMP headquarters, I started to realize I could be deported immediately. Lilith was still in hospital and the children were here, and I would have been deported without making any contact with them. They would have been left in limbo. So when this officer started to make out my chart I insisted I was not illegal. He became very annoyed. Finally they said, "Okay, let's go home to see your records." On the way they were still trying to make me say I was illegal here and asked me if I knew any other people who were illegal too. I didn't answer them. When we came into the house I showed them my passport. "How come you told us your name is one thing and now you show us a passport with something else?" They were annoyed. I asked them if they would believe me or the passport. This made them even more annoyed. But now at least they knew that I was not illegal in the country. They had to change the charge from being illegal in the country to working illegally in the country, which is not as serious.

Afterwards, they asked me for Lilith. I still wasn't too definite of their mood and I told them she had met with an automobile accident. I said what had happened to her hands. Then they discovered that we had two children. They asked me what I was going to do. I admitted later on that it was an industrial accident that had happened at the same company. They were furious again, not because I had tricked them but because I had never reported the accident to them. The company had never reported it either. The company couldn't care less about what happened. So the immigration officer told me I was very stupid not to report the accident. He said I would lose all my rights. "What rights do I have?" I asked him. "I have no rights in Canada." But apparently whether we were working illegally or not, once we had a job we were covered by Workmen's Compensation. Anyway, they took the passports and they locked me up. They locked me up at Parc-des-Neiges lockup. I had to go to court next day and pay $50.

LILITH: This was just before my final operation.

AUBREY: When they let me out it was a Tuesday. On Thursday I had to go back again to Immigration and tell them I was going to school. They didn't want to believe it. They couldn't understand how I could go to school all day and then work eight hours. This puzzled them. However, the interrogation ended abruptly and they allowed me to go. They haven't troubled me since. Not directly. But the RCMP came to me once and they asked me to work as a trap to catch other companies. They would use me and pretend I was an illegal immigrant, then they would raid the company and have living evidence of the company hiring illegal immigrants. I told them I was a bit doubtful about that.

Then they came back and asked me if I would testify against Trans-World. I said yes and both of us gave them statements. Since then, things are a bit quieter now. The man from the RCMP said he would tell Immigration not to worry us until everything was settled. He gave me a work permit and I have a job now in a textile factory. I weigh out the dye for the materials. I earn the minimum wage – $2.87 an hour. The work conditions are bad. It's always damp. I don't think it's anything they can avoid. You work with a lot of steam. There's condensation between the cold air and the hot air. This creates a vapour which forms water which keeps dropping all the time like rain. I start at 7 in the morning and finish at 4:30.

I had to drop out from school for a while because of the accident but I'm going back in January. When I start studying again I might be able to change my shift to the night. But I don't know. Nearly 90 per cent of the people working there are Haitians.

LILITH: Right now, the most important thing to me is that now that the hands are healed I want to go to the Rehabilitation Institute and get whatever they are supposed to give me and do something. I want to go back to school to finish off my course. To get the hands and finish off my course.

AUBREY: We'd like to be able to stay in Canada and be able to bring our other two children. They're now eight and five. We would like to stay in Canada for many reasons. It's very difficult to explain. I don't see Canada offering anything more than my own country would offer, if I decide to live according to the conditions that exist in my country. When I was at home, I earned $200 a month. I was able to live quite comfortably because . . . well, I didn't have four seasons to contend with. And you can walk through the rain. But the political climate is such that it's becoming very, very difficult. People of my age, because of direct involvement with the political situation, prefer to stay in Canada than go back home. Those who go back run the risk of being put in jail or sometimes an attempt is made to assassinate them.

I even find it difficult to accept the fact that I want to stay in Canada because of this. I have become so accustomed to speaking out. I find it goes against my conscience to turn my back on the situation. But then I console myself with the thought that I am one man. What can one man do?

Lilith, student, and Aubrey, student

13 Dealing with Immigration

When first you arrive the immigration official looms all-powerful. To be accepted by Immigration is to be accepted by Canada. You are not always certain what acceptance will entail. Whatever it is, you usually feel you have no option but to go along with it.

Allowed to exist

We came here because a travel agent in Colombia convinced my husband that it was a good idea. Canada is a rich country, he said; they need immigrants. Buy a ticket, look around for a while, then if you like it you can stay. It seemed very attractive. We saved every penny we could for about 14 months, then we sold our house, my husband's tools and the beat-up van he had put together from old parts.

It was like a dream we used to talk about all the time. I think everybody in the little town where we lived knew about our trip to Canada. But I don't think I really began to believe it until a couple of months before we were to leave. When my husband came home one night and said he had made the reservations on the plane, I felt as if I were hearing about it all for the first time. I cried and cried that night and felt that I could not leave my sisters and my parents. First my husband was angry, then afterwards he put his arms around me like a child. I knew what he was saying was true. We had to leave then. Everyone was expecting us to leave. Most of them had never wanted to believe us in the first place. If we decided not to go they would say forever that we had never any intention of going, and that they always knew. . . . You know how it is in small towns.

My mother said she would keep the children until we were more settled. In any case, there was no money for us all to come. At one stage, I even thought I should stay until my husband got a job and found us a place to live. But he wanted me to come with him and I'm thankful that I did. I've seen so many men who have come alone. After a while, loneliness makes them a bit mad, I think. Women and drink, that's all they think about. So that by the time their wives come, there is no marriage left.

Near the end we got quite excited. It was true there was no future there in our own country for us. My husband had a small mechanic shop that he operated with his old father. It wasn't much and there was no way it would ever get better. At least in Canada the children could go to a good school and we could earn good money and save, and if we wanted to go back after four or five years, we'd have something really solid behind us to buy a business.

At the airport in Toronto we got our first shock. We found out that what the travel agent had told us was not true. We were not allowed to stay in Canada and look around to see if we liked it or not. We waited at the airport in a special room for many hours. I was very frightened. We told the truth and how we had saved to come but the man did not seem very interested. I was grateful the children were not with us. They are very small, and I know they would have been very afraid.

In the end, the man from Immigration said we should come back in 10 days to the airport again. I kept thinking of that travel agent in my country. I wanted to kill him.

It took us nearly two years to become landed immigrants. And I think we only were successful because of that amnesty in 1973. If they hadn't decided then to let us in, we would never have had enough points. Even though we still had to wait until our appeal came up, I'm sure it was a change in the regulations that helped us.

Sometimes at night in bed we used to talk about what we would do if they decided to deport us. My husband said we would go underground and just stay there. We know lots of people who were here illegally. Somehow it didn't seem fair. We had tried to be honest all the time with Immigration. We went back to the airport when we were supposed to, and we did all the things they told us. And we had to wait a long, long time for our papers. Some people had never gone back to Immigration when they knew they would be deported. They became afraid and knew that it was important to get a job. So they just went underground. And these people could get the amnesty. We know many who had their papers long before us. That made us start to think about the Canadian form of justice.

When the children came, we had been apart for nearly three years. I was full of fear that they would not remember me. All that time we had sent many letters and photos to them, and my mother and sister would do the same from there. They were shy for a few days, but they were pleased to be here. I felt as if I might burst the day they arrived. It is not easy to be separated from your children.

I miss the political life here. There does not seem to be any way we can join into it. Our English is not good enough to join a group of Canadians to do anything. And we have not had too much success trying to make our immigrant friends interested. The pattern of life for many immigrants does not allow too much time for doing things on a long-term basis. You work, you eat, you care for your children and then you must start again to work. Part of you changes and dries up. You are not whole anymore. It is as if you are here to do what you can to be allowed to exist.

Julieta, office cleaner

Housewife

One of the first things that annoyed me about Canada was the attitude in the Canadian embassy in Tel Aviv. Not only did they not ask me what my profession was, but they obviously had no interest at all in what I did. It was something that really bothered me. When the immigration officer asked me what I intended to do in

Canada I said I wanted to work. He told me that in any case he would write down "housewife" because it would be easier. I said all right because I wanted to come and I didn't know any better. I realize now that it was a mistake. That is how the bureaucracy works. But it is important for women to insist they be treated as individuals, too.

Beatriz, education worker

The greatest country in the world?

We came here in '69 not really knowing anything about Canada. We'd been living together for some years but were not actually married. However, we thought it would be easier to come into the country if we were married. This turned out to be not such a good decision. If we had not been married I could have come in independently as a landed immigrant. But being married to a student I could only come in on his student visa.

We were given very poor information at the consulate in Chicago. They told us that I would be able to get working papers and that I'd be able to get a job here. But in Canada we discovered there was no such thing as working papers. Either you're a landed immigrant or you just starve. So I scrabbled around. I did get permission to work part-time. I got a job marking papers at UBC. I also did some work at the library school as a typist, and then I got a part-time job for a business firm. Essentially, I was working all the time. But nothing ever connected up. I was really frustrated.

When we did go down to Immigration to make application to become landed, I said I was the head of the family, that I had the skills that had been supporting us for years, that I spoke both French and English. They laughed and said no. When I insisted that I was the worker, they just wouldn't accept it. It had to be my husband. The head of family had to be male. And his chances were not nearly as good. I don't think the immigration official liked us very much, but he was decent with us. He explained that if he sent our application to Ottawa it would not pass and we would be deported. So we withdrew our application. We were still here on a student visa.

The next year we got ourselves together and went to a man who had been working with draft-dodgers. He gave us a lot of information. He told us, for instance, that we shouldn't go to the downtown immigration office but that we ought to go to an out-of-town office where they very much liked married couples. We got all dressed up. I put on heels and everything. My husband shaved off his beard and cut his hair. They were very pleasant to us. My husband had a job offer that didn't really apply in the country but it showed we were respectable. Someone had offered him a job as a managing editor of something. But they couldn't have cared less about us and we just zoomed through.

We'd never done anything like this before, but at that moment, it was simply expedient and I didn't mind doing it. What I had minded was the attitude of the man in the downtown immigration office where we had first applied. All he wanted us to say was that we hated the United States and that we loved Canada, that we thought Canada was the greatest country in the world. But we explained to him that we couldn't say that because we hadn't been here long enough. We didn't know the country. That was why we wanted to apply for landed immigrant status. We wanted to find out about Canada and how could we find out if we were not able to stay? But he wanted that kind of affirmation immediately.

I said to him, "I admire Canada. You're helping draft-dodgers and I think that's very admirable. But I can't say I love this country because I don't know it." It was the principle of the thing at that point. We weren't about to tell him all kinds of lies. The second time we were prepared to do it, if necessary. But they didn't demand it and I felt much better about Canada that they didn't.

Linda, trainee printer

We deserve a chance

My husband was very active in his union in Guatemala. He was one of the representatives chosen to work with the government to try to get better work conditions. Then one day we received a letter from a group that terrorized trade unionists. We were very frightened. They warned him to stop his union work or he would be stopped. We knew what that meant. In our city there is a river that flows through the town. There are stakes sticking out of the water of the river. Sometimes in the morning, there were bodies on those stakes. They never found out who did it. No one ever was brought to trial for those crimes. So when he got that letter we were afraid.

He told the company where he worked about it, but they did nothing. A second letter came and then suddenly, the company told him they did not need him any more. We never knew for sure, but when he could not get another job, it seemed as if his name was on a list and no one would hire him. He had become known as a representative of the workers.

In Canada, it has been trouble all the time. He came alone in the beginning. Immigration told him he must go back to Guatemala, but he made an appeal against the deportation. It took a long time for his case to come up. We couldn't come, the children and I, and he was not to leave the country. But after more than two years, I came to be with him. He told me I should not come but Immigration finally decided I could stay until his case was settled.

The papers finally came through and Immigration said "No." We could not stay. We have a lawyer who is trying to help us and we had to pay him $700. It is a lot of money but it is very important to us. We have five children in Guatemala with my mother. They have to eat and they have to see their father. They have not seen him now for almost three years.

In our own country there is no work for him. Here, he has had a good job at the same place for over two years. He earns close to $4 an hour, and with my job at the restaurant it makes it possible to send money home for the children. We must be allowed to stay. We deserve a chance.

Celia, dishwasher

Landed

I came illegally over the border. I didn't have no papers or nothing. I was in the back of a car. I explained to the people I went over with what had happened to me. They knew everything. I had my sailor's book and my passport all laying in my suitcase, all opened. The people I was with, they told me, "Now you lie in the back and just loosen your tie. If Customs opens the car, we'll just tell 'em you had too much to drink." So I just lay in the back of the car. The guy opened the door and said, "What's the matter with him?" "He's had too much Seattle," they told him. And he just waved us through. That's how I came into Canada. That was in 1947.

I arrived on a Friday. My brother-in-law asked me, "What are you going to do?" I didn't know, so we picked up the paper and there was a job in the paper in the cement business. He warned me it was hard work but I went down on the Sunday morning and the guy hired me. At that time they had the old streetcars down here, the old streetcar tracks. So they give me a jack-hammer and I worked on that for six months. Taking out the old tracks. Was that hard work! When you came home at nights you were still shaking. But I got $2.85 an hour which was pretty good pay then. No one ever asked me for papers. Every year I filled out my income tax, sent it off to Ottawa, and it came back and I got my return. Nobody ever asked me anything.

Then a doctor who lived across the street from my sister, he never liked it that I was working on the cement and everything. I used to go over in the evening and play ping-pong in his basement. He said I wasn't built for that kind of work. I was quite a bit lighter 30 years ago than I am now. He asked me if I'd ever worked in a hospital. I told him "no" but said that I'd worked in a restaurant and done a bit of cooking here and there. A week later he gave me a piece of paper and told me to go and see this man and he'd give me a job in a hospital. This man was the chief orderly there. He gave me a uniform and said, "Okay. You go up to the operating room." I wasn't expecting to go and work in an operating room. The first month it was bad, but after that it was good.

There was one doctor, an anaesthetist, who asked me one day where I was from and so on. We got to talking and he said I should go down to Immigration and so on. In the meantime I had got married. My wife was expecting. That's why he said, "You should go down and at least get a paper so you can stay in Canada. Otherwise they could ship you back any time." He promised that if anything happened I should just phone him and he'd stand behind me. So I did that. I went down to Immigration. I had to fill out deportation papers and the next day we had to go down to the board of inquiry. What was in my favour was the fact that I had five years of a steady job in the hospital.

It wasn't too long before they sent me out and said I had to get character letters. Quite a few doctors in the hospital gave me letters and the two chaplains also gave me nice letters. I was back two days later. The immigration guy was quite surprised. "You got them off in a hurry, eh?" he said. Then when he started reading them . . . .

About a year later they sent me back all my papers with my landing card. I was a landed immigrant. Thirty years later, I'm still a landed immigrant.

Jan, retired

A beautiful body

So a lot of people look down on me for what I done. I ask them what they would do if they were in my shoes. I was a nothin' in Jamaica. Just a poor coloured girl. A domestic girl. My mother had a lot of kids and we were very poor. My father he didn't live with us. And it's probably just as well. He's a cruel, sadistic man, my father. He grew up in a cruel environment. So he just turned out cruel. It happens to a lot of blacks.

Anyway, I managed to break away and I came here. I didn't have no money. No job. No status. Nothin'. So I go into this immigration office and this man says to me, "Why don't you take off your coat, honey. Why don't you?" I don't want to take off my coat. But he says, "You ought to, you know. You got a beautiful body." So I know immediately what he's after. And I don't even care about that much. I mean, what's a bit of sex if he can help me with my papers. I don't want to go back be a domestic all my life. I mean, I want to make something better of myself.

So he helped me. Oh yeh, he strung it out a bit so's I didn't know if I was coming or going. But every time I'd come in to see him we'd fix a time for him to come and see me and make it out with me.

I'm not ashamed. He was no better, no worse than all the other men in the world. And when I got my papers I finished with him. Yes sir, I didn't have to any more. I'm working now doing trays and things in a hospital. And a friend of mine is tryin' to help me get a job as a cocktail waitress.

Annette, hospital worker

14 The whole world upside-down

Nothing is the way it used to be before. The most ordinary things are different now. It confuses you. It makes you feel depressed. It makes you angry.

Squid

It is not easy to live in a new land at my age. But my daughter and her family are here and I like to be with them, especially if I can be of some use. I went to English classes but it was very difficult. My tongue and my head are not built for the strange new sounds. The first six months I was here, I didn't get onto a bus or a streetcar alone, I was so afraid. My whole world had been turned upside-down. But I got by. I remember wanting to surprise my daughter by preparing her favourite dish – squid cooked in its ink. I had seen a fish market one day when we were out together.

The next day, when my daughter went to work, I set out on foot and followed the streetcar tracks for miles downtown to where I had seen the fish store. I took a can of squid that we had in the house and somehow managed to make them understand I wanted fresh squid. When I got what I needed, I then followed the car tracks back to the house again. Can you imagine that? I followed the car tracks on foot, rather than get in the streetcar and have the driver say something to me I would not understand. But it was worth everything that night to see the look on my daughter's face when she saw what I had prepared.

Victoria, babysitter

Near death

I feel fulfilled here. I have a job in a factory. It's not a very good job but I am able to help my family financially and that makes me feel very good. My husband is a chemical engineer but he does not speak the language and he must work here as a welder. I have two children now and I am grateful for this. I was pregnant when we arrived and lost the baby two months after we got here. It was a bad time for us. All the problems in Chile both after the coup and then when we managed to get out were too much for me to handle, I guess.

Just a few months after we arrived here, our eight-month-old baby got sick. It was so cold outside that we were afraid to take him out. We thought it would make him worse. All day and night he cried with stomach cramps and diarrhea. We were very worried but we had no idea how serious it was and there was no one to ask. Finally, we managed to find a Spanish-speaking doctor who hospitalized the baby immediately. He said that because of the diarrhea the baby was losing all the fluids I was giving him and he was severely dehydrated. He told us that within another two hours the baby would have been dead. Can you imagine how we felt?

Cristina, garment factory worker

Day care

As a community worker who is also an immigrant, I've realized that one of the most serious problems every immigrant working mother faces is day care. Only this week, something happened which demonstrates just what a problem this can be. A Peruvian woman who started work two weeks ago in a day care centre came in to say that she couldn't take it anymore. She had to quit. She then told me an incredible story. The very first day she arrived for work, she realized that there was something very strange going on. The day care centre was in a house in suburban Toronto. All of the children, 50 of them, were down in the basement. Twenty-eight of the children were under two years of age, the youngest was three months old. The tiniest babies were sleeping in the laundry room alongside the washer and dryer without any heat or light.

The children were picked up each morning in two vans and a station wagon by the husband of the woman who runs the centre. He would start picking them up first thing in the morning and have the three vehicles at the house by 7 o'clock. This was a terrific thing for many immigrant mothers who have to leave home very early themselves to get to the factories where they work. The whole operation was done very carefully. All the vans had curtains, so that not even the neighbours knew who or what was inside them. The vans drove right into the garage and the children were taken from there directly into the basement. They didn't go outside at all.

This woman worked there for two weeks and, in all that time, the children were fed spaghetti every day for lunch except for one day when they had rice. The fruit and cookies that they brought from home were taken from them, the idea being that everyone had to have the same food, or it was not fair.

Unfortunately, this Peruvian woman is illegally in the country. Actually, it was because of this that she was hired. The people who ran this place are themselves Latin American, from Uruguay. They said that they understood the plight of people here illegally and wanted to help. They also said that they wanted a Latin American because she would best understand the habits of the immigrant children. When she was hired she was paid $70 a week to work from 5:30 in the morning to 7:30 at night. Fourteen hours a day! It means she was being paid a dollar an hour. Besides her and the woman who ran the place, there was only one other person working there, an Italian woman who was paid $70, too.

It seems incredible that they could have operated this place with the neighbours having no idea all those children were in the house. The only thing they knew was that every day very early in the morning the vans drove in and at the same time every afternoon, they left again, curtains drawn. The neighbours had no contact at all with the occupants of the house.

As soon as I learned about it, I called the Day Care Administration and within half an hour they had an inspector visit the place. This inspector was a public health nurse for North York. As soon as she got there she realized it was the same address she had been given about a month ago in another complaint. Someone had phoned her denouncing the place but refusing to give any name or identification over the phone. At that time, a woman had answered the door and had told her there must be some mistake because they were in the laundry business. There were no children to be seen or heard so, thinking it was a crank call, she had let the matter drop.

This time, however, when she went there, she knocked for 15 minutes before a man eventually opened the door. His story was that they had moved there only three weeks ago. But the inspector realized that the van parked in the driveway was the same van that had been parked there a month ago when she visited the house. She asked to see around the house, but he refused. When she asked about the basement, he said it was rented to three men and he could not allow her in without previous authorization. So she told him she would be back the following day to see the basement and asked him to make sure he got the authorization.

When she got back to her office, she realized that it had not been very smart to warn him that she would be back, so she went right back to the street, but this time to a neighbour's house to see if she could see the children leaving. However, it was 5 o'clock and all the vans were gone.

The incredible part of this story is that most of the parents had taken their children there because they were referred by other parents. When parents first enquired about the place, they were shown the upstairs part of the house and were told that only five children were taken care of. As far as I have been able to find out, none of the parents had any idea how many children were there. The place was clean, the woman very friendly and then there was the big bonus of the fantastic pick-up service early each morning. They must have been very convincing, because so many parents were taken in. And since the children were too young to talk they had no way of letting their parents know how badly they were treated there, how they were slapped and hit when they didn't do what they were told.

It's interesting that one parent I contacted had withdrawn his child from the place some time ago. The little boy used to cry and cry every morning before being picked up. One day, a woman who worked there told them not to send him any more, that it would be much better for him to go somewhere else. But she never gave them details and refused to say anything more.

It is a frightening story. But for me, the most frightening detail is that the six-month-old daughter of a couple I knew died in this very same house three years ago. This means we have proof they have been operating for at least this length of time. The baby had been left there in the morning (again, the mother understood there were only five children being taken care of) and then during the day the baby was found dead. There was an autopsy and it was said to be a "crib death" – one of those sad, unexplained things that do sometimes happen. This whole new situation probably means nothing more in the death of that baby, but it does add a macabre note.

When the inspector went back the next day the place was locked up. The people had disappeared without a trace. The house is now under police surveillance and the matter under investigation by the authorities. The house was licensed only as a "supervised home" and not as a day care centre, so they had no authority to have all those children there. They were making a lot of money. They were probably clearing well over $4,000 a month. And unfortunately, they were immigrants exploiting immigrants and using children to do it.

Evelyn, community worker

Now I would hit back

One day, my wife and I and a friend went with our English class to see the museum on Citadel Hill. It was a hot day and I was very thirsty. I wanted to drink something, but there was nothing around. My wife's friend had to go to work at the furniture store where she had a job. We drove her there and near the store was a restaurant. We went into the restaurant, and I asked for three cups of tea and a coke extra for myself because I was so thirsty.

The waitress said that it was dinner time and we would have to order something to eat. I told her that I didn't see any sign on the door or the table saying this, so I didn't see it was necessary. No one could push me to buy something to eat when I was only thirsty. Finally, the waitress said she could not serve us. I asked who was in charge and she said she would ask the woman behind the counter. She asked her and came back again to tell us she could not serve us and we would have to leave. I went over to the counter and asked the woman there why she wouldn't serve me the tea. She didn't even want to talk to me. "Go out. Go out of the restaurant," she said. I told her, "Excuse me, but I am not a dog."

There were many people in the restaurant and she spoke to me in a very loud voice. It was a bad situation. I asked then for her name. I thought there must be some kind of businessmen's association to whom I could explain the situation. "I don't want to give my name. Just leave the restaurant," she said. At this moment, from the kitchen came this big Greek. And he hit me. I fell all over the tables and chairs onto the floor and cut my fingers. They were bleeding. I wanted to hit back but my wife came between us and told me not to do anything to him. I went across the street to a phone to call the police.

In very short time the policeman was in the restaurant. He asked if anyone had seen what happened. There were very many people in the restaurant, but nobody saw anything. I felt terrible. It was mid-day in the middle of the city and it seemed incredible somebody could just do this to you. It was the first time anything like this had ever happened to me. The policeman said he could not do anything about it but he said if I wanted to I could go to court and say what happened. Oh, there was another important detail, too. After the Greek hit me, when I still did not want to leave the restaurant, he said to my wife, "If your husband won't go out of the restaurant, I'll kill him." That was when I went out to call the police.

I went to the Manpower office because I needed information about where I could get help. They sent me to Legal Aid. I went there and got a young lawyer. Finally the case came up in court. I told my story and my lawyer questioned me, my wife and her friend about what had happened in the restaurant. The Greek was there with three lawyers – all of them very experienced. They didn't question me much. They hardly asked me anything. But when they questioned the Greek he now had three or four witnesses, people who were working for him. All of them said he had not touched me but that it was I who had hit him. It wasn't important because I don't think the judge believed it.

But the lawyer then began a very good play. When first he took the Greek on the stand, he asked him to tell a little of his history. Of when he had first come to Canada. He came 18 years ago. He was poor. He had no money with him. He worked very hard. Today, he has been able to buy a house for $100,000. He has a big restaurant. How hard this man had worked for what he had. And now along comes a new immigrant and he gets help to learn English. Canada pays him while he learns. He is just looking for trouble.

I lost the case. The judge said he felt that I was too sure of my rights. I was with two women and he understood I wanted to show off to them. Because of that I was pushing the situation.

Today, I don't believe in justice. If somebody were to hit me in the street, I would hit him back. I know now nobody will look after me. It has made me realize that here I must have money. With money, you have power. Without it, you are nothing.

Maciej, clothing salesman

A whole new language

I remember once hearing a tale about a Hungarian chap who came out. He was told that the first thing he has to do is learn English. So he goes into the bush with a logging crew and stays there for a year. When he comes out he's very pleased with himself because he has not spoken one word of his own tongue and has learned a whole new language. But imagine his surprise when he found out he still couldn't speak a word of English. It was Finnish he had learned!

Eli, retired

Cucu, cucu

We went through some pretty rough times here. But you have to start somewhere. Not speaking the language made it much more difficult. I could have bought some stuff on credit – groceries, something for the kitchen. And then I could have paid it off when I got the money. But I didn't have the language to ask.

We starved quite a bit. With no reason. There's no reason to starve in this country. But we didn't speak the language and there was no way you could go in and ask for help. I remember the first store we went into here to buy groceries. We wanted eggs. Oh, my God, how to explain? Finally, we had to do this, "Cucu, cucu, cucu." *(He bends his arms and flaps them like a chicken, all the time roaring with laughter.)* I'm not kidding. We had to sit on a box and "cucu, cucu." It was the only way. The only way.

Odilio, machine operator in sawmill

IV

MAKING
IT

15 Gerry:
I got it made

A tavern in old Montreal. Draught beer. A Claude Leveillée recording fills the background, but no one listens. It is all noisy talk and laughter. We do our share, too. When Gerry laughs he puts back his head and just roars. He enjoys life. He has confidence in the way he controls it, too. Proudly he shows me a picture of his wife and son. Then he pulls out a picture of his cab – a big, American car, clean, well-cared for. Every inch of it is his.

I work here for a long time after I arrive, doin' this job or that job. Never had a problem 'cause of the language. I knew quite a bit of French when I came. Quite a bit! (*He laughs.*) Seriously though, even if I did not come from France you quickly learn the language when you start to work. You got to understand, to keep gettin' that pay cheque. So you understand fast. Fast. You learn what you need to know. Nobody likes to starve.

So I work first at this thing. Then at that thing. For a while I get a job loadin' at a warehouse. But I wreck my back after a while. I'm not used to it, you know. And it kills you if you don't know what you are doin'. So I quit it. I don't want to kill myself or make myself good for nothin'. I quit and go on a delivery run for a small grocery. But it's not much money, eh? The work is not hard, but the money is bad. It's no money for a married man and by now I'm gettin' married.

You see, there's this girl I met at a dance up in the Laurentians. She's a French-Canadian and she's nice, eh? Nice enough so I decide the girl I am engaged to in France should stay there. So I write to her and say that things are pretty rough here and she ought to stay in her own country. I say it but it is not the truth, eh? I mean, I never had a problem here. Like I said, I had a pretty good knowledge of the language and the rest I learned pretty fast. But I kind of felt it is nicer to say to a girl, "Look, you're not gonna be happy in a new country without your family where it's hard to make your life," than to tell her I met someone else and I don't want to marry her. But she was eager, eh? She keeps writin' to me and beggin' me, beggin' me, beggin' me. So I just quit writin'. I change my address and I don't tell anyone. I don't want problems, eh?

Anyway, pretty soon my wife and me we have this kid, a boy, and we move to a duplex. You want your kid to grow up in a decent place, eh? You want him to have toys and a bit of space to grow in. So we get this place. Nice. Three bedrooms, but a big rent. Still, I'm happy about it, eh? I mean, I want the best for my wife and kid. But it means more furniture, more this, more that. Next thing you know it's big bills every month. We got to pay off the charge accounts, the loan at the bank, the car. I get a job then runnin' a gas station for a friend of mine. But I'm there all the time. The money is not bad but it doesn't do anything to my bank account. My wife and me we start yellin' all the time. Always at each other's throats. It's always problems in the house. The kid is growin', but the money is always tight.

So then I get this chance to go up to James Bay. They're takin' on people and they want a truck driver. I sign on for a year. It's not a bad life, eh? I mean there's about 400, maybe 500, guys. We live in a pavilion – two to a room. People think you go up there and rough it, eh? But it's just the same as livin' in Montreal. They got a tavern and they keep it open all day. They open it in the morning for the night shift and at night for the day shift. Same with the movies. A movie every night, a movie every morning. The food, it's all right, eh? I'm not gonna say it's like what my wife cooks. I mean my wife is really a good cook. But you wouldn't expect it to be like home food. I mean, you eat in a restaurant and it's okay, but it's not good like what you make in your own kitchen.

They tell me up there that I can come down every two months. But I don't come down until I am there a year because I know that if I come down I will never go back. I work seven days a week. That's a lot of overtime. And when I don't work, I read. I do a bit of study. I taught myself English up there. I was in a room with this guy could speak good English so I think, "What the hell!" and I learn it. So now I can go to Ontario, eh, and get a job there, too.

They don't let you work seven days a week any more. No more than six days now. They don't want to pay out no more money than they have to. But it's good money and drivin' a truck there, it's no harder than drivin' a cab in Montreal. Only thing I got to do is pull this lever and I drop the back and unload the rocks I'm movin' from there over to here when they're blockin' it all off. I was happy up there. Like, I'm the sort of guy can be happy with a newspaper or a book, and the guy I was roomin' with, he was decent. Sometimes we'd go have a few drinks or see a show. He was decent.

The worst thing was I didn't see my wife and kid. That was the worst. But after one year I come back with enough money to pay off a few thousand dollars debts and buy myself a cab. I bought the whole thing – license, meter, light – just the whole cab complete. What do you think of it? It's a nice job, eh? Paid cash for the whole thing. Now I'm on my own and I ain't never gonna work for no one else. No more. Why would I do it? I work 12 hours a day. I get up at 3:30 in the morning. I get dressed and get into the cab. I don't say I'm happy to do it. Like this morning it was very hard. I didn't want to get out of my bed at 3:30. But you do it. You got to make a livin'.

And anyway, those guys who work in an office, they work eight hours. Sometimes even nine hours. They spend one hour gettin' to work, one hour gettin' home. Even more, if they live way out of the city. They get one hour for lunch. No one pays them for that. So that's 11 hours, 12 hours maybe. In 11 hours today I already made $85. How many guys in an office make that kind of money? I'm my own boss now. I got a nice house, my own car, a good wife, a smart

kid – and no bills. Nobody tells me what to do. I'm on my own.
That's what I like about Canada. You use your head, be prepared
to work, and you got it made. Just like me. I'm tellin' you, I got it
made here.

Gerry, cabdriver

16 Naomal:
Flotsam and jetsam

A big, split-level bungalow in suburban Calgary. "It was easy for us," Nao
tells me. "All the houses were new and the neighbours were all just moving in.
We didn't have to integrate into an already settled area."

His long dark fingers meet together as he talks or run through curly black
hair, showing its first vague touches of grey. He is excited by Peter Newman's
The Canadian Establishment, *which he has just finished reading. We*
talk for a while about Canadian politics and the structure of society here. Then
while Deanna fixes supper, Nao and a friend put together the telescope he
bought his seven-year-old son for Christmas. "This is very relaxing," he says.
"The wonders of the universe are unreal."

To be honest about it, I would have preferred to go to England. As
a young boy in Ceylon I had a voracious desire to be a barrister of
Lincoln's Inn. Various factors prevented me from doing that. Looking back now, I think my whole desire was politically motivated.
All of our leaders were either from the London School of Economics
or were barristers of Lincoln's Inn. So I suppose remnants of this
idea were still there and I wanted to go to England. But unless you
were qualified technically, it was very difficult. The only English-
speaking place I could get into was Canada.

It was a very difficult decision for me to leave my country. My
cultural background was such that we were very attached to the
family. We were a very, very tight unit. Maybe it's difficult for a
person in the West to understand this, but even a grown-up child, a
son, always lives at home. If he marries he brings another member
into the family. The daughters go out. When they are married they

124

go with their husbands. But the sons stay at home. So that it was difficult for me. It came to the stage that even my mother decided it was best for us to leave. You see, due to various changes in government in the country, there was more stress laid on the mother tongue and on people who were educated in the mother language. I was one of those caught in the interim period. I was completely educated in English. I found myself suddenly faced with the prospect of switching over to my own mother tongue which I didn't know except to speak and read a little. But I couldn't write. So with this switch-over, I found myself in the middle.

I thought that I could blossom out into my full strength and make use of all my aptitudes coming to an English-speaking country. I worked for the Ceylon Fisheries Corporation – a Crown corporation. Coincidentally, this Crown corporation has been aided almost 100 per cent by the Canadian government in the matter of trawlers, offices, equipment – the whole works. The two of us, my wife and I, worked there. She was a secretary and I was a publicity officer. In the last 10 months of my stay, I got involved in trade union activities and they suspended me.

Just one week before we left in 1972, the government imposed a regulation under emergency stating that all emigrants would be allowed to take only $100. I wanted to go to Toronto. I think that's the dream of every immigrant. But I didn't have any money. So my only option was to come to Calgary where my wife had a brother, establish myself a little bit financially, and then move to Toronto. But once I came to Calgary, I liked the place.

They speak of culture shock. I had never experienced it until I came here. Calgary was the antithesis of everything I had ever known. The first thing that struck me was disillusionment. I thought, "My God, my English is not good enough." I couldn't make myself understood. I was asking for "trousers" when they were saying "pants." Then I found that they couldn't speak the language themselves, using the double negative and so on. So I ended up putting myself in the situation where if I speak with a certain kind of guy, I use the double negative myself. "I do not know nothing." But I wouldn't want to say that to a guy who has some education. It's a question of adapting myself every day to very rapidly changing circumstances.

I had to get employment. I didn't want to be a burden on my brother-in-law. This is a bit unusual, it is quite unlike the Ceylon mentality. There, families live together. But I didn't want it. Maybe a certain little amount of pride. Maybe also, thinking of the other guy, that I would be putting him to trouble. So I went into this place call Domtar Packaging. Most guys that came here from Ceylon seemed to get a job at Domtar as their first job. And most of them stayed on there. Domtar was "open sesame" to all and sundry from Ceylon.

This was another shock. I had never done manual work in all my life. And then came my thorough disillusionment. This is not your average type of factory. They get every ounce out of you. At that time, I joined at quite a good wage. They were paying $3.66 an hour. It was unionized, and that's why the wage was good. I was a labourer taking off these beer-cases. When they were cut off from the machines, I'd have to take them. I considered myself up to that point a very hard man. An emotionless sort of guy. But I used to cry. Tears would roll down my face. I was feeling sorry for myself. Then began an amount of degeneration in my life. It was the first sign of danger. It caused me real problems. It caused me to drink like hell. I used to get drunk every day. I used to want to drown this damn situation. Culturally and socially, there was no outlet. And there was no going back. You were a social outcast. If you went back you would be this guy who couldn't make a go of it in Canada. So it was demeaning to go back.

But one day I knew that either I had to quit or to go back. I had a friend back in my own country who had told me, "Any time you're in trouble, I'll pay for your tickets to come back." But I was very confident and sure of myself. I was cocky. I had said, "It won't happen." I was 36 years old. I had never done a labourer's job in my life. I was not the epitome of physical fitness. So I thought, "Damn it, I'll quit." I was considered to be a very good worker; this was the contradiction. As a matter of fact, they kept giving me more and more jobs because I was damned good. I made a point of hiding my true feelings. The bosses liked me. The manager had already told me that this was not the job for me but just to be patient. He had already written to all the other Domtar plants to see what he might be able to get me. But none of the other plants were having any vacancies to fit me. So when I walked up to one of the bosses and said I was quitting, he asked me what the hell I was talking about.

There comes a time in a desperate situation when you are devoid of all feeling. I think it happened to me at that time. I was like flotsam and jetsam. I just existed. I didn't live. I just survived. I quit and drew unemployment. But I didn't like it. My friends used to say, "Look, you might get into a job where for 30 years you'll be paying into Unemployment and not drawing a penny, so don't feel badly." But I did feel badly.

I became aggressive and only then did something start to happen. I had to do something. I was a drowning man. I came here with a lot of hopes, and I could see my future going down the hill. I was drinking a lot. It was causing problems at home. My young son was scared of me. My whole world – the castle I'd been building – was falling right around my ears. And I didn't like it. I just couldn't cope with it. I brought a case against my Manpower counsellor and said she was discriminating against me. There was an inquiry and, of course, they asked me to drop the charges and said they would see what they could do to help me.

After the inquiry, the manager of Manpower told me they were willing to allow me an exploratory grant to go anywhere in Canada in search of a job. Now, up to this moment they had never showed any interest in anything like this. Only now that I had become aggressive did I seem to become eligible for this money. "Go anywhere in Canada to see about a job. We'll pay for you and your accommodation. Once you get a job, inform us and we'll pay for your wife and child to go there, plus your furniture and other belongings." It was bloody good. They asked if there had been any place where I had already tried for a job. I told them that I had already applied to the Alberta Liquor Control Board. I had passed a test five months before, but they still had not called me for the job. Now, only two days after the inquiry, the Alberta Liquor Control Board called me to say I had a job!

Then things were okay, but I was still drinking. I had started to go downhill and there was no stopping. I had to face that I must stop drinking, and finally I did. That eased a lot of my problems. I was mentally more alert. I could see things clearly. And one of the first things that struck me was that I wasn't doing the job I was suited for. As long as I was drinking I didn't give a damn, as long as I had money to drink. But when I stopped drinking, I realized that this was part of the problem. A void was filled by the job, but as the days rolled into months and the months rolled into a year or so, I was getting frustrated. It was a matter of pricing bottles, putting bottles on the shelves and putting big brown bottles into little brown paper bags. I was not being fulfilled. I wanted to change jobs.

This is something I thank Canada for. You know they say the best of steel goes through the harshest of fire. I have been through an ordeal here which has been a very valuable experience to me. I have come to know more about myself and to understand that you cannot live without fulfilling a good part of yourself. There have been some beautiful people among Canadians who have been there when I needed help. More than that you can't ask of any place in the world.

Now I've applied for the position of inspector at the liquor control board. It is a job which will give me a certain amount of intellectual stimulation. But they called me last week for an interview and told me they can't give me the job because I am not drinking. As an inspector you have to go to bars as a decoy, an undercover man, to see these guys and nab them. It's very ironic. The way I was drinking, they would never have given me the job. Now I've stopped drinking they still won't give it to me. It's very frustrating.

I'm not sure what I will do now. I have tried to consider what I feel to be my assets. But I have had to accept that some of these assets are not regarded in the same way by Canadians. I am being charitable when I put it this way. The people here may not understand my accent, but, and this is perhaps more important, they do not like my accent. I am old enough to know resentment when I see it on somebody's face. And I come, more than most other people, into contact with a cross-section of the public in my work at the liquor board. I see them all from the top to the bottom.

One day, for instance, I was on the till and this young university student was my wrapper. A guy came up and there was resentment written all over him. He just glared at me. I was extra careful to be extremely courteous to him. "Thank you very much, sir." "How are you, sir?" He didn't utter a word. He took the bottle and said to the young guy who was wrapping, "Why is it that you can't be on cash and get that guy to wrap for you?" The young student didn't know what he meant. All this was foreign to him. He started to explain to this man the schedule we work to. "He's not interested in that," I told him. "He wants to know why I'm not doing more menial work because of my colour." This young guy working with me was stunned. All he could say was, "The son of a bitch."

This gave me another insight. Many Canadians themselves have no idea of the feelings of other Canadians toward us. This is something that most immigrants are faced with. The confusion that exists about race, about colour. The idea that you have come to enjoy what someone else has sweated for. But we're making a contribution, too. God damn it, we are.

When I walked down the streets of Ceylon I walked, literally, with my head held high. I knew this was my country. Now, when I walk down the street here, I can see in the other guy's eyes: Here comes an immigrant. If I live another 200 years here I'll still be an immigrant. It will not be based on my accent. It will be based on my colour. I keep getting the message, "You are not wanted, buddy. You will be tolerated, but you are not wanted here."

Naomal, liquor control board employee

17 Stella: Domestic

Montreal, caught in a blinding snowstorm. It has taken me a long time to get a cab and then to reach the attractive suburban duplex. It is nearly noon. I ring the bell and get Stella out of bed. She is tall, slim and walks carelessly with an easy grace. She talks without difficulty about herself and her life here.

This second place I worked was terrible. Well, I wouldn't say it was just terrible. I always think that when somebody does somethin' for you, you owe them a favour, kind of thing. 'Cause that's life, you know. But I did go through a lot. I did have to see psychiatrists and all.

I was like the wife in the house, I would say. I didn't consider myself a slave in her house because I did it freely. The only thing is, in my mind, I was a slave in the beginnin' because I couldn't get my stay in Canada. I couldn't leave there because I wasn't free to leave there. I had to stay and go on with the different kinds of stupidness was goin' on there. I'd get up in the mornin' around 6:30 or sometimes 6 o'clock. By 12 o'clock at night I'm still up on my feet. Sometimes even later if they have guests. I lived there, of course, so if I didn' feel like goin' anywhere, I didn' go anywhere. And I didn' know anybody for about six months. So I was always just there.

It was a terrible experience because she was very fussy. And I know that when people are fussy it can be a big strain. But she was a very open person which made it very nice. And then for food or anythin' I didn't have any big difficulties. But she depended on me for every single thing. She did nothin'. I did everythin'. I was the wife, the maid, I did the homework with the kids, sometimes I'd sleep with them in their bed. I'd cook. I did everythin'. She depended on me for everythin'.

For a time there it was terrible. But after a while you have to get used to it. She is the kind of person who . . . uh . . . open marriage. She was always talkin' about "open marriage." We spoke about everythin'. Guys used to come in there – her friends. They'd make passes at me. Her father attacked me. Her brother-in-law attacked me. Her friend did it one time. This is the thing I had to put up with. I couldn't do anythin' about it because she was the type who thought that if somebody attacked me, well, I was pretty and I should accept this sort of thing. They would make passes, grab me to kiss me, feel me. I would gently push them away because it was, for instance, her father. I never actually told her about her father. But I did tell her niece who was much younger. Though I never even told her that I was friendly with her uncle, the woman's husband. I didn' even tell her that. I did tell her that he was fresh and makin' passes. And she said, "Oh, I know that."

I never had problems there with my own friends. They'd always say, "Bring them in and give them somethin' to eat." And compared to some of my girlfriends who were workin' in houses I didn' have such a bad time. But it was hard. I did have slight mental problems because of all that. It is a trap situation. The husband was always talkin' about sex. Behind her back, of course. He would be very affectionate. But it goes on in the family, this affectionate business and she didn' take any notice of that. I don' think that she knew we slept together. I'm not sure that she knew that.

But he did bring me a drink one time and this is how he started. He started makin' passes. And he started bringin' in the favours that he done for me. He likes doin' favours for people, he says, and he likes them bein' returned. He didn' say it in the exact words but he said it. And I said to myself, "Look, I'm not a landed immigrant and I don' want to go back home because my life there was not very nice. (I wasn't married or anythin' and I had a son.) I may as well stay. What's a little bit of sex?" But I hated it. I hated every minute

132

of it. It makes life a bit difficult. If you do somethin' you dislike, it always makes life very difficult.

He expected it would continue after the first time. Sometimes she'd even be upstairs. And I'd be downstairs. I didn' have any private room or anythin'. I had my own room in the basement. You know, the basement go down the stairs. So they come through the garage and there's my room. I felt like I was a slave, for that reason. I wasn't free to say, "I would like you to leave me alone." You know, even when I was goin' to leave them he was mentionin' that he did me a favour. But the wife she was not. She was sayin' that she hoped I get somethin' else.

Being a servant was my main problem. Who would like to be a servant? Domestic work is a hell of a thing. It's okay if you're free to go and clean up and leave at four. But when you have to sleep in and have to ask everythin' like – Can I use the phone? Can I do this? Can I do that? Then it's bad. But I lived there a year and a half and it wasn't so bad as the next-door neighbour who had a domestic who was my girlfriend.

It's very common for girls doin' domestic work to have to have sex. I think that it's human nature in the first place. I think that men are curious for black girls. They want to see if it will be different with them. And for some reason history, I don' know what it is, has always said that black people are very good with sex. It's just junk of course. But still they just want to know if it is really true.

I always used to have these crying spells. I was very skinny at that time, very depressed. My back-home experience was always comin' to me. That I'd had a terrible life and that everythin' was always goin' to be terrible for me. At one time I thought I was goin' crazy. Well, I was takin' drugs at the time, and she knew this and she was more scared than anythin' else. So she sent me to a doctor.

To meet people was the hardest thing when I came here. And I keep tellin' my sisters this. I have three sisters who came on a holiday and they stayed a while. I was tellin' them how hard it is to make friends when you're here alone. They had me so it was easy for them. Once you know one family it is not so bad. My first friend that I made here was a taxi-driver who was black. But I used to go out a lot with the niece of the woman where I worked. I used to go out with her and her friends who were all white. They were very young, and young people seem to be different for some reason. They are very curious people. There's always a little bit of curiosity in black and white. How do you get your hair like this? What do you do with this? And so on. I guess you can't get away from that. But they weren't as . . . . The guys, for instance. A young boy wouldn't make a pass at a black girl unless she was young like him. He might even marry a black girl. But an old man. He'd be dirty for no reason whatsoever.

When I came here I left my son with my boyfriend's mother. That was another thing that was responsible for my emotional problems, too. I found it very, very difficult to leave him. It was the thing that hurt the most at the time. He was only two and he was just a baby. And I couldn't help but worry about leavin' a baby like that. I'd think, "I wonder when I'll get to see him again. Maybe he'll be 10 or something like that." But I saw him when he was three. My boyfriend brought him. He stayed and we got married.

My life before was not very nice. If it was, I wouldn't be here. I was doin' domestic back home, too. I think what made me accept my problems a bit more here is that I was used to this in Trinidad – my domestic business. But with white men in Trinidad, there's no problem. They're not fresh. They never made passes. Maybe because they're more prejudiced but they don' even know why. If you really prejudiced you don' sleep with a black girl. 'Cause then your bodies are joinin'. I think the people there are much more prejudiced. They think it isn't clean to sleep with a black girl.

I figure this is a white man's country. This is how I look at it. I feel angry, but I don' feel angry with this country. To know that in my country the white people are always on top, even though they are in the minority, this is what hurts. Here, the people they choose white people to live here. And we is just here. We might get thrown out one day. I'd much rather be in my own country, but the economic situation is so bad there. It's terrible 'cause in Trinidad there is a lot of money there. But the government . . . . Here, there's room for improvement, there really is.

For instance, the girls who went through the problems with the immigration guys, having sex with them and all this business. If I was in their position I would not condemn the guys for what they did. Because there are situations in Montreal like where, for instance, my boss slept with me. It's the same thing. The only thing is I cannot go and expose him for what he did. It wouldn't make any sense. I did it and I did it because I wanted somethin'. And I feel that people are doing so many stupid things in this world. Like to go and expose a man.

It's worse for the people right now because the immigration department, the officers, they're rough with the majority of the immigrants right now because of this, to try to get back at them somehow. For instance, now they can come into your house and search, pick you up in the street, say you are not an immigrant and arrest you. It never used to happen before. They use some devious way to pay off for what happened to the other officers back there, the ones who were exposed. Those officers want to sleep with those girls because they're just like other men. They probably said, "Look, I like you. You've got a good body. And I'm givin' you somethin'. There's no harm in givin' me sex in return." It's up to the girl. When she gets her paper or whatnot, she doesn't have to see him again. I have a lot of friends who went through the same deal. I even had a girlfriend who went into sleepin' with guys to get money. It's like the same thing. It's like prostitution, as a matter of fact. You help me and I'll pay you off in this kind of way.

This black thing is a big hang-up. Not only for whites. The blacks have got it too. It's a kind of inferior feelin'. I guess it started back centuries ago with the slave thing and the blacks from Africa. Now it starts to get to be a kind of class warfare. The blacks from Africa on the bottom, then the island blacks are considered a step up, but they are not as good as the Canadian blacks. And, of course, no one is as good as a Canadian white. Being black you learn to accept a lot of stuff. A whole lot of discriminatin' and exploitation. But it's goin' to change. I jus' don' want to be part of the change. I have had a lot of problems in my life and I don' have the strength. And it takes a whole lot of strength to be a black these days, and to make somethin' of it. But whether I'm part of it or not, it's goin' to happen.

Stella, unemployed

18 Bruno:
A good country
if we take care of it

The edge of Prince George. A long country road. A large wooden house about 60 years old. Dorothy and a protective German shepherd greet me at the door. I am ushered into an enormous living room. Bruno is busy with a German carpenter who is going to build them some furniture. I enjoy the chance to explore the room and its fine wooden ceiling. It is near the end of January but an oversized Christmas tree still stands decorated in one corner. Dorothy explains there hasn't been time yet to take it down.

She shows me photos of the house and how they had it moved in two pieces from the other side of town. When Bruno comes in he tells me proudly, "Canadians wanted to tear this place down, but we moved it. They were amazed it could be done."

I was a dairymaster. My intention was to stay in my trade here. I went to Ontario and got a job in a dairy farm in Markham. I didn't speak English when I first came here. I could say "yes" and "no." The farmer I worked for was a German. That's why I came over to him. He had advertised in a German paper. So I had the job before I came. I could communicate with him entirely in German. But right away, I took evening courses in a local school. It took me about half a year. Even then, I didn't speak fluently English, but I knew enough of the basics to get by. The rest came automatically then.

After a year I decided I wanted to see Canada. I didn't want to sit forever in a little farmhouse in Ontario. I wanted to see what the opportunities were. I didn't like that part of the country anyway. It was very flat and everything was square. There was absolutely nothing that attracted me there. I had heard about the west so I took a trip out here. I had read in the *Star Weekly* that in a town called Prince George immigrants were making plenty of money in the woods, so I decided to go to the woods myself.

I came here to Prince George and went immediately into the woods. I'd never worked in the woods. I didn't know what the woods meant. I became a canthook man. That meant I was rolling logs in the bush. And I was doing pretty good. The pay was considerably better than what I'd been earning. I was getting about $1.45 an hour and I was working about 10 hours a day – two hours overtime. Before, I'd been getting only $75 a month, with free board and room, of course. Here, I was getting free board and room, too. I think you paid only $2 at that time, and you got excellent food. So I stayed in Prince George. After a while I got into lumber piling in the sawmill. The pay was even higher because they paid you $1 for every thousand board feet of lumber you piled. If you were able to pile 25,000 board feet a day, you had made $25. I worked the night shift as well. On the night shift the same two-inch lumber was then re-sawn again. They paid me another dollar a thousand, so I could make $50 a day. $50 a day. That was, in 1952, a tremendous amount of money. Building lots, 60 by 120 feet, were selling for only $25. So you could buy two building lots per day.

This was a young country. There were plenty of opportunities. There was no way that you couldn't find work. In 1953, there was a long strike for five months. I went to Vancouver. It was hard to find a job but I found work carrying sacks of coal all day. It was a hard job. A dirty job. With the rain in Vancouver, the coal juice is running down your back and in the evenings you look like a black man. But that's the way it was. You could always find a job if you wanted to. I was used to hard work and long hours. I was used to being dedicated. Nobody ever fired me. I had to quit sometimes in order to see another place.

I came to Canada for the one and only reason that Germany was over-populated. With all the destruction of the war there was very little future. Here in Canada there was such a small population that a man had more of a chance to acquire something. With the wages we were getting and with the frugality of the life I was leading, there was definitely a chance that I could acquire something. One day I was in the beer parlour. It was spring breakup. That's the time when the snow is melting. The ground is soft and they don't log in the bush. They lay all the men off. It was an annual affair every spring when we were laid-off for eight weeks. I had decided to go to Vancouver and look it over. But I thought I'd have a last drink in Prince George. I ran into a fella, an old bum, and he sat down to get a free beer out of me.

He told me he was a feller. Now the fellers were the big shots here. They were making the big money. I had never felled a tree so therefore I couldn't go into the bush and fell trees. But he was a feller. He had nothing, but I had money. I forgot about Vancouver and bought a power saw and we went into the bush felling together. We had to wait eight weeks until the bush opened, so we worked in the mill here. When the bush started up again we went felling. He showed me how to fell trees. You got about $1 a tree at that time, and even with those clumsy power saws that weighed about 35 pounds, you still could get about 70 or 80 trees down and earn $70 to $80 a day. As the saws got lighter and the efficiency of the saws improved, we were able to fell 100 trees a day, or even more. Now, of course, they fell considerably more than that. But at that time there was the 18-inch limit. That meant that no trees under 18 inches were felled. Nowadays they go down to seven inches. But then, you had to take a wide area just to find the bigger trees. The smaller trees you left standing.

If my father would have been with me when I first came up here and went into the bush, he would have cried all day to see the timber that was wasted. We took only the biggest trees that were growing in the interior. The little ones with only 10-inch tops, they were

139

chopped down and just left there in the bush. Many trees were run over with the big machines and broken in half. And when you felled a big tree it usually smashed through the other trees and knocked down some smaller ones. Sometimes those trees were fair-sized, but they were too small. They were below the 18 inches. They were all left. There was nothing taken out. So much waste. Over a period of time, say the last 25 years, when I go back into the forest, I see how we have destroyed it. That's one area where I have to criticize Canada. They thought they had a kind of spring there that was inexhaustible. But now people are beginning to realize, it runs dry very fast. It takes a good tree 200 years to grow. And they talk of harvesting trees in 80 years!

I was felling for two years and then I decided to have a trip back to Germany. Good friends talked me into starting a business there – a small laundry – which was a failure. I came back to Canada. I'd lost all my money. Everything I'd saved – about $10,000 – went down the drain. It just didn't pan out. I went straight back to Prince George and bought another power saw. I went back into the bush and kept on felling. That was when I made up my mind definitely to stay in Canada, regardless of what others might write about how business was good again in Germany. People said this from their own point of view. It was better for them but it really couldn't compare with Canada. When I went back there I realized there wasn't much in Europe for me. I stayed in the bush for two years.

Before, I'd never spent any money. I lived on a dollar a day. You could do that then. I had a little shack, eight by eight feet – and that's where I lived. At that time pork chops were still about 50 or 60 cents a pound. So you bought a pound of chops and you could live on that. Most of the time we ate in the bush anyway. But then I bought a flashy car. It was a Meteor. Whitewall tires. Automatic. I had met a guy who came from Germany two years earlier. He went to Calgary, got a job and bought a sailboat. He wrote to me inviting me to visit him. He wanted to show me his sailboat. So I thought, "Okay, I'll show you my car." I drove to Calgary to see him. When I arrived there, his wife, who was a nurse, had invited this friend of hers over to meet me. The rest is, of course, history. *(He laughs.)* We got married and came back here to Prince George.

When we started out I bought a mobile home and a trailer. It was very small – 8 by 22 feet. That's what we lived in. It was very cosy. Of course it wasn't insulated. The walls inside froze up to a height of four feet. It was so small. There was too much condensation inside, and it showed on the walls as frost. It was warm enough. You just couldn't go close to the wall. We sold the trailer a year and a half later. Then we bought a little house. Unfinished, no basement, an outhouse, a few miles out of town. "Shiplap" they called it. It had only rough lumber nailed on the outside. We put in inside plumbing. I made a basement behind the house, then we lifted the house up onto it.

We never had any debts because we paid everything as we went. As we made money, we finished off the house. In three years it was all finished off, landscaped and all, and all paid for. I worked day and night landscaping it, and my neighbours were quite upset. It was the only house on the street that was landscaped. My neighbour came over and said, "You better stop that." I asked him why. "Because my wife keeps saying, 'If you'd only work as hard as he does we'd have our place nice, too'."

When that house got too small, we bought this place. It was supposed to be burned down and destroyed, you know. They wanted to put a street through and this house was sitting smack in the middle of the right of way. We bought it for $250 – that was the total price – but it had to be moved right across town to this land here. We'd bought the land before. There was no access to it when we first got it. Nothing. Just a little cabin down by the river where an old-timer lived. Seventy-eight years old he was. He wanted cash. That's the only reason he sold his little one-room shack. In the summertime we lived three months down here by ourselves in the shack. That was the only time you could make it in and out. It was

141

beautiful. Then one day they built the road in, so we could move this big old house from town.

To me that's the big difference about being an immigrant. A Canadian thinks this country owes him a living. Whereas the immigrant comes over very insecure. The only security he gets is when he can save some money. So he saves his money. He keeps every penny. He doesn't like to go to finance companies or to mortgage companies to borrow. He sticks within his needs, at least for the time being. And this gives him an edge over the Canadian. From my experience now that I'm in real estate, I can say that a young couple, they want everything. They go deeply into debt. Then to meet the debts they have to make so much money. Whereas the other man who has no debts he can work for less, but he can go ahead. And that's what we did.

Stamina – that's what a man needed up here. You go in the bush and it's 30 below with 11 or 12 feet of snow. You go from tree to tree. The wind is howling though you don't feel the wind so much with the trees around you. Your wood is frozen. The wedge that you put in will hardly stick into it. It's all like glass. You have to be very careful then. It's very dangerous. But in order to make money you can't afford to be too careful. You have to go fast. If you fiddle around with one tree all day you make nothing. You have to get the trees down. You do that day after day – snow, rain, whatever. You go out there first thing in the morning. In the evening when you come home you fix your saw up again to get it ready for the next morning. Then the same thing. Get trees down. Count every time a tree goes down as a dollar or 75 cents or whatever that goes into your pocket.

You do it in the summertime when this country is loaded with mosquitoes. You sweat, and the sweat is running down on you and the mosquitoes bite you. Then your senses finally get dulled and you don't feel the mosquito bites any more. Then there's the isolation. Even when we were married I was usually a week gone. I only came home on weekends. So my wife had to manage alone for the weekdays. Sometimes, we'd work five days, sometimes six, or even seven. It all depended on how they needed the trees. Sometimes I was even gone for 14 days. I didn't even show up on the weekends at all. That was one of the tough parts of it.

This is my home now. It's a good country if we can take care of it. Immigrants will still come for a long time to Canada. Nature doesn't allow a vacuum. It won't allow empty spaces when other countries are over-populated. So there'll still be a steady stream. Maybe in times of economic slow-down, not so many will come. But then afterwards, we'll have a boost of economic activity and they will pour in again. That, of course, is one way of beating the unions. The immigrants usually work for less and so they have a surplus on the labour market to hold the union in check. This is strictly a political matter.

They're going to have to stop the growth of the big cities, though. They're going to have to disperse the people in areas where there is plenty of growth needed. We are people that are still only one or two hundred years away from our basic roots – which are in the land. Now suddenly, we have become landless people who live in huge, big apartment blocks completely removed from the earth. Those people are unhappy. They get sociological problems. And it's all a question of greed. As cities grow you make a fortune on land. You don't have to be smart. You just have to invest in land and you get rich. (If you have the money, of course.) Stopping the growth of the cities is all we have to do. We don't let them become uncontrollably large. We make smaller cities – 150,000 maximum. We know from experience that a city of that size has enough tax money coming in to have the cultural amenities that it needs. When that size has been reached we go into new areas and disperse people. If we were to build satellite towns strategically connected by highways we wouldn't have people living in one area with big empty areas everywhere else.

There's still this old pioneer spirit here. "I own a piece of land. I can do with it what I want." But I say "no." When it comes to other

things maybe you can do what you like, though in a complex society we can't do what we like anyway. But when it comes to land we
are not owners, we are only custodians of the land. This land must
be preserved to nourish the population.

Bruno, real estate agent

19 David: Independence

David is friendly when I come up the steps and into his home. But his black eyes watch me carefully. A dark, bearded man with two deep scars on his face and long, sensitive fingers. I sense he has interesting things to tell me, but it takes time to break through his caution. Finally, he says how he hates the way immigrants are exploited here. Especially domestics. He'd gladly support any friend rather than let her do domestic work and be exploited.

He puts on a record of his 100-piece steel band, winners of the 1976 championship in Tobago. The music is joyous and full of vitality.

You is sunk if you's not independent. I been independent since I was 16. I worked two weeks in a rum factory, bottling rum to pay for my passport and my papers. I got $4.31 a week. Then I signed on a ship and sailed to Port Alfred. I was the first one in my family to go to sea. I wanted to travel. I earned more money as a kid at sea than mos' men workin' on shore. Don' ask me why they ought to pay you more. But they do. That's jus' how it is. Anyway, nobody works to make money. Only them what's born into it make money. That's the way it is.

After a few years on the ships I come into Canada in '68 and I decide to stay. I like it. No big thing, y'know. I jus' get off the ship and stay here. I left Halifax and came to Montreal and I been livin' here ever since – same address, same place. Mainly I stayed on here so long because at the time there was a long dock strike. And there were no more ships. That lasted mos' of a year. I never bothered with anythin'. Always had a job, kept out of trouble. I used to do

145

odds and ends. I work here, work there, paintin', doin' the odd job, part-time at Hudson's Bay. But I had money then, y'know. When I came in here, I was supportin' myself a few years.

Then Immigration found me in 1973. I don' know how they found me. When they came to get me, I wasn' afraid. I knew they were gonna come one day. They came and knock at the door. I was sleepin'. I jus' came from work. They ask me my name. Y'see, they went to my nephew here first, he was landed. And then they ask him about me and where I lived. Then they came. Just two of them. No uniform. Two RCMP. They were nice enough. Then I went up. They kept me in a lock-up for three days, four days. I had a special inquiry. I put up a bond of $300. But eventually I did get everythin' back. It didn' take too long to sort it all out. I worked on it and had friends work on it. I even went to the *Guardian* and the *Gazette* to write up about it. They didn' give me any trouble and then I was landed. It didn' take me long. But it's different now. It's quite hard for those what come now.

I still work on the sea. I jus' came off a ship 13 days ago. I been at sea now for 25 years. I enjoy it – gettin' around. But it's gettin' hard to get jobs on the ships now. The air transportation is takin' mos' of the work from ships. Right now, I been shuttlin' between Havre-St. Pierre and the northeast of Canada. Before that I used to run off the Great Lakes. Last time we were away some 26 days. We were carryin' ore. You make pretty decent wages on board ship. You work eight hours a day and you can work overtime. But even then, it's not like what you used to make before.

I'm registered with Local 41 of the Shipworkers' Union and now I wait 'til they call me. They have a seniority list. When they can't get the senior men, they take what they can get. There's work right round the year. The Great Lakes close on December 15, but there's some ships go to Europe right through, and to the United States. I'd like to get a shore job now but there aren't many jobs around any more. Especially at that sort of money. Then too, there's a problem here. It's a bilingual place and I don' speak French. On the ships, the language is no problem to me. I always get along. But if I had to go to some other place in Canada now to get a job, I jus' couldn't do it. I mean, I been livin' here all these years and I know this place now. It's my home. I mean where you sleep is your home, eh?

Canada's nice. I like Canada. But bein' an immigrant is pretty lonely. It's a lonely life. First you got to get adjusted. I don' like the cold. And the longer I stay in it, the more I get to dislike it. Then too, I'm out here alone. All my family's back home. I got a big family. So you get lonely at times, eh? It really isn' worth it.

Before I went back to sea last time I had a nice job with Hudson's Bay. I was a stationary engineer. I would call it a janitor work. But this wasn't really a janitor work. They had boilers and things. And I been experienced in these things all my life workin' in the engine room. I'm not qualified with a piece of paper, but I know what to do. So I had this job there and when they decided to make me permanent, I was faced with a big problem. My boss who didn' know nothin' is comin' and seein' that I know more than he knew. Then, he started to go on. And I tol' him off and I quit the job and went back to sea. It was a pretty good job but to be honest you don't get no good wages up here. Not for the cost of livin'. I make more money at sea. When I go to sea I work by the hour and the more hours you work the more you make. I still feel I'm capable of workin' at least 12 hours a day. I'm used to it. I can work long hours. In any case I got to make myself quite a bit of money. Got to support my six children back home. That's the main reason I stay here. Unemployment is bad. . .very bad in the Caribbean.

I don't have much friends here. It's not that I'm a private person. At times anyone would be happy to sit down and talk. But there jus' isn't anyone there. Some folks think you get lonely at sea but I don' see it that way. You can' do two things at once. When you're workin', you're workin', and when you're playin', you're playin'. At least that's the way it seems to me.

David, seaman

147

V

FAMILIES, CHILDREN, FRIENDS

20 Rosanna and Marino

A small, well-kept bungalow. I had come early to talk to Rosanna before Marino arrived home. But today, he comes early. She smiles, but continues to talk freely about herself and her life. She is very much the mistress of her household. A beautiful young woman with long hair. No make-up. "No wife of mine is going to go around with stuff all over her face," Marino tells me later. Rosanna laughs out loud, shrugs and says, "You see the problems I have." But her gay, independent manner tells me that the compromises between them will not be all in one direction.

Rosanna

My mother always said to me, "You're not cut out for the farm, to work in the fields. Maybe if you're a good girl somebody will come from America and want to marry you." It was like a dream that I grew up with. So when my husband came along, I said to my mother that she had got her wish.

He was engaged to another girl in his home town, 10 kilometres from where I lived. But then he started to have second thoughts. He had a cousin in my town and his cousin talked to my mother about any girls she knew. She told him that the only girl she knew was me. She said, "She is very young but I will let you meet her. However, don't put your hopes too high." So he came and I met him. I hated him the first time. To me he was just an American with a pocket full of money ready to buy me off. I didn't know what he wanted.

Then my mother told me that he wanted to marry me. I remember I was holding a book and it just fell out of my hand. I thought, "So he wants to marry me and he's not even man enough to come and tell me to my face." I didn't even want to see him again. But my mother begged me to be polite. He came to supper that night and told my father that he liked me. "If she agrees," he said, "I'll marry her tonight." My father looked at me and asked, "What about you?" I shrugged and I guess he took that for an answer. And that was that.

We knew each other only two days then he came back to Canada. We started writing to each other. I was a little bit afraid but he was so understanding and so nice. And my mother, who really had met him more than I, was convinced he was a nice guy. According to her it was really something to be a girl going to Canada to be the Mrs. of somebody. So it became exciting for me. In six months I came over to my mother-in-law's house to be married. A little bit at a time after I married my excitement failed. All the hopes that I had went down and down. After I was here two or three years my hopes started to grow again. It happened when I started to know the country, its size, its people, what they believed in, when I started associating with them all. But for a couple of years I was out. I was in Canada but I didn't belong here.

Everything seemed so strange to me. When you are young everything is so strange. And I was so young. I turned 17 one month after my wedding. It was a different way of living here. A different way of everything. It seemed funny to see the houses painted in every colour. Back home, they are only of brick. I came right to Halifax. I stopped in Montreal to change planes but then came right on here. I spoke no English at all when I first came. I felt I was in a dream world, walking on the street and not knowing what people were saying to me. I went two times to English classes. But by that time I was pregnant with my little girl. My husband travels a lot back and forth around the city and I decided not to go any more.

When you don't understand English and you don't know your way around the city, it is difficult. But gradually you start to go out with friends, the TV helps and you find you are starting to adjust. I didn't find it as difficult as many other people do. Maybe they are quite a bit older, or they have quite a lot of sacrificing to do because

151

they came with a young family. For us it was a fresh start. We were both young. We didn't have it hard at all. Oh, it was hard because of the language and to adjust myself to the climate and the people. The people here seem so much colder than people back home. But I always felt I was in a golden cage. I've got gold, I would say to myself, but I can't touch it. It's not mine.

When I had my little girl it was horrible. I still couldn't speak any English and I used to mark everything in the list they gave me for food. I didn't know what it was. But I made myself understood. It was only nine months I had been in Canada but the people here are so understanding. They look at you funny when you can't speak 'cause it's harder on them than it is on us. It was difficult to understand what the doctor said to tell him, where the pain was and so on, but not as difficult for me as for the poor people who had to help me out. My little girl did not start to speak English until she was five and she started school. We spoke Italian all the time at home. The first month at school was difficult for her. But after that she was my teacher. If she had had her way she would have talked Italian all the time at school in the beginning. Now, if she had her way she wouldn't speak Italian at all. They change.

The children have a better chance than I did when I was little. They are freer. If they need something, there is always somebody to help you here. Here they respect you for what you are. If you need some money and you have a good job, you go to the bank. You get it. Back home it is difficult to do that. A farmer can't get those things. You are always in a lower class. So I've decided that if my children can have a better chance because we live here, I will sacrifice anything I can for them.

Rosanna, housewife

Marino

My mother came here first. Then my father, myself and two brothers came about four months later. I was just a kid – 13 years old.

Things were tough in Italy. Though we were all right. We weren't rich but we weren't starving or anything. There was enough to eat. But my family came and I really didn't have much choice. Things were very different then. Immigration was just starting up. In 1957 there was very little immigration going on. I didn't know we were coming to Canada. The only thing we heard was that we were going to America. I remember one of my teachers asked me once if I thought I was going to come here, load up my bags with money and then go back. But I never thought that. You've got to work wherever you are.

My mother had relatives in Halifax, that's why she came here. We probably would be better off now if she had gone to Toronto or Montreal. I never heard the word "English" before I came here. I couldn't understand the other boys and went through some bad times at school. When I came here they put me in grade seven – the equivalent of what I had done in Italy. When I went into grade eight I couldn't read very well so they put me back to grade one. Little kids were sitting all around me and there I was trying to learn how to read and write. I was 14, going on 15 then. I was angry, but then I felt it must be for my own good. I spent six or seven months in grade one, then I started in grade seven again. When I finished grade nine I went to trade school.

I started working when I was 14 years old – during the summer. I was working at a construction company as a water boy. I made in a week what my mother and father earned together. Then I worked weekends and nights at a restaurant soda fountain. I was still going to school. My father wanted me to go to college. But things were hard enough for me. I couldn't see myself going through college and passing. I thought I'd just be wasting my time. When I finally did quit school after grade nine to go to vocational school, I'd been on the honour roll for three years. But I had to work for it.

I wasn't lonely though. I was too busy. I was the eldest. My parents and my brothers depended on me. We bought a house after we were two years in Canada and I was doing all the repairs in the home. I was too busy to run around with the gang. My father was working in a laundry. My mother worked there too at the laundry of the Halifax Infirmary. When I finished vocational school I was 22. I was a trained automobile mechanic. I had worked at my trade during the summer and the manager liked me a lot so I had no problem finding work. I had work before I even got out of school.

Making friends was hard everywhere. Even at vocational school, 16 of us started a three-year course and I was the only one who finished. And when I did finish the course, at graduation night I was given a $250 purse of tools for the best improved student over the three-year term.

I didn't know many girls. I didn't like the night life – drinking, dancing, going to clubs. I always used to be home by 11. I don't enjoy smoking, drinking, sitting around with the boys. I'd rather be working, doing something. Just sitting around talking bores me. That's why it was harder for me to make friends. I wasn't a drinking buddy. I used to hear Canadian guys talking of how they did the dishes, how they did the cooking. I wasn't going to put up with any of that. That's a woman's work. God made woman from the rib of a man to be his companion. If I couldn't have it my way, I wouldn't have it at all.

I went to Italy for my grandmother's funeral. I was engaged to someone but I met Rosanna and I decided to bring her here and marry her. I wouldn't mind helping her when she's sick, but I'm not coming home to do all the housework. My mother always worked hard. Anyone can tell you that most Italian women work hard, both inside and outside the house. But they still do all the women's work. That's the way it is in Italy. That was the way I wanted it in my family. I know a lot of Canadian men and they work hard all day. Yet the first thing they've got to do when they get home is slap on an apron and cook dinner and do the dishes from the night before. What kind of a life is that? The way you make your bed is how you're going to sleep in it. So before you make it you better think good about it.

Marino, elevator inspector

154

21 Marriage

It is a good feeling to have someone beside you. To not be alone. But sometimes, the pressures of adapting to the new country put unbearable stress on the complex relationship between a woman and a man.

We are all together

We are now all together in Canada – my husband, the children and myself. But it has cost us a lot. When my husband came here he took all the money we had been able to save. It wasn't very much but he needed it to buy his ticket and have something to live on while he found a job. We thought then that the children and I would be able to follow him within six months. Nobody told us that the Canadian immigration laws would be so hard.

My husband was ordered deported. They said he could not stay in the country. When he wrote and told me, I was sorry I had not been with him at the airport because I am more aggressive than he is. He is a very quiet man and will not always fight for his rights. But he was able to appeal the deportation and they let him work, too.

After one year, when still he was writing to me sending some money but telling me he could not bring us yet, I began to get suspicious. I tried to get him to come and spend Christmas with us at least. The children were missing him. He is a good father to them and the oldest boy needed him around. You know, a boy of 15 without his father gets hard to handle. Anyway, he told me that he was not allowed to leave Canada until his case came up and was settled.

I was having problems myself with the children and my family and, to tell the truth, I imagined that he was having a good life in

155

Canada and sometimes I would imagine maybe he had another woman here and was lying to me. Then one day he phoned to say he was accepted as an immigrant and we all could come soon, but first we must get married properly. I didn't understand him and he told me that in Canada they had said I was no relative of his and unless we got married and adopted our children he would not be able to bring me.

This was a bad moment for me. In the beginning, I thought he was using this trick to leave me and the children in our own country. I could not understand it. You are with a man for 16 years. You take care of him, bear his children, take care of his sick old father and then they say you are nothing to him. I did not react well. He had to come down before I would agree to it. He came down for a month and I could see then he was missing us as much as we had missed him. It was not all easy in Canada as I had thought and he had worked very hard to send us the money every month. But still, Canada was a better place for the children to get an education and have a hope of a job.

I agreed to get married. But even then it took us more than a year to sort out all the papers. We had to adopt our own children as if they had been brought into this world by other people. We are all here now but it has not been easy. There seem to be too many times in your life when, just to go on, you must give up a part of your spirit. I am not certain it is worth it.

Delfina, garment factory worker

Marriage and passion

When I first came here I met an English girl. She was a hairdresser, too. We became very close friends. We worked together and even shared an apartment until she got married to an Englishman. Not too long after that she died of cancer. I knew her husband well. We had been like brother and sister. After his wife's death, he asked me to marry him. I liked him and respected him and realized there was more to marriage than passion. I saw the good qualities of the man. He is easy-going and has such warmth and love in him. I decided that I would marry him and though we do, of course, have some problems now and again, he has been a wonderful companion, lover and husband to me.

Our marriage is not the same as an all-Japanese marriage. It is not the same as a white Canadian marriage. But I think it is a good one. My husband is a remarkable individual. He was a seaman for many years. People are people to him. Even when we went back to Japan for a visit he managed very well with my family. The only thing was he was so much bigger than everybody else!

Toku, housewife

Our marriage was over

I had a very bad feeling the day that my husband left to come here. I think I knew then that it would be a long time before we would be together again. What I don't think I realized was that it would never be quite the same again for us.

At first when he was here and he would write and say not to come yet, I thought he was just putting me off. I even began to think he didn't want me here with him. It's not difficult to think things like that when you are alone and lonely. But then last year he said that he was a landed immigrant and could bring us all. When I heard that I came immediately. I didn't even wait to do all the papers and things you are supposed to do. Fortunately, Immigration let me in. My husband said anyhow he had already made the application to sponsor me so I suppose they didn't feel it was too serious.

For a few days it was exciting to be together. It was like being on a vacation. He showed me around and was full of attention. But then I had to look for a job, and he was off all day in the factory. Sometimes, he didn't come home until very late because he says he must work overtime every week. We have to send money home for his parents every month. So far I haven't been able to find any real

157

work. I'm cleaning in a big house two days a week and one night I do some serving there for receptions and dinners. But it doesn't earn me too much money.

Last week, I got really fed up with him and we started to fight. I'm pretty sure he is with another woman a lot of the time. I can't prove it. You can tell though when a man is really with you, when he wants to be around you. And most of the time he acts as if I don't really exist. He's angry with me because I haven't found a proper job and whatever I do is wrong. He hit me and hit me the other night. I had to go to the hospital the next day, mainly because of my eye. It was so swollen that I couldn't even open it. But I didn't tell them what had happened. I said I fell down the stairs.

He said that if I told anyone he would not sponsor me. He'd say that our marriage was over and he just didn't want me to come in the first place. And I've got to stay with him. I'm going to have a baby.

Lola, domestic

Valentine's Day

Last Valentine's Day I turned 23. It was one of the worst days of my whole life. I had been to the doctor that morning and he had told me that the baby would probably not arrive for another two or three weeks. I was so disappointed I started to cry. I had put on a lot of weight and I just felt so big and clumsy and fed up.

When my husband came home that night I hadn't got dinner ready or anything. I was just lying on the chesterfield watching TV. I didn't feel like doing anything. He started yelling at me and screaming and telling me I was like a pig, that the house was never cleaned properly, that I never got his meals ready on time. As he got madder and madder with me he started accusing me of worse things. Then finally he yelled that probably the baby wasn't even his.

158

That did it. I'd sat quietly through the whole thing until that moment. To tell the truth, I'd felt a bit guilty. After all, he had been working all day and I hadn't done a thing but go to the doctor. But you know, I just couldn't move. I was fed up and tired and disappointed. Anyway, when he said that about the baby, I couldn't stand it anymore. I'd been a virgin when I married him and I'd never even looked at another man, and he knew that. So I started to pound his chest with my fists. He just laughed at me and flung me across the room. Then he got a chair and threw it at me.

I was frightened then, thinking of the baby. I started to scream and he just walked out of the house. I didn't know what to do, so I called my mother after a little while. She came over in a taxi with my father and they took me home. They were mad as can be with my husband, calling him a brute and everything.

The baby was born the next day and I wouldn't see my husband for three weeks. I went home to my parents' when I came out of hospital. Then, one night my father said I really should go home to my husband. He said that I had no right to deprive the baby of her father – that I was my husband's wife and he had a right to have me living in his house. I wouldn't listen to him; I felt all mixed up and upset.

After that night, my mother started talking to me and trying to convince me. Finally, I've come back to him. He was pretty mad with me in the beginning, but then he really liked the baby and things seem to be better now. I don't know what's going to happen to us. I have tried to understand why he did that to me, but I don't understand. I don't think I ever will.

Marriage isn't what I thought it was going to be anyway. But there didn't seem to be anything else to do. You grow up in an Italian family and you're expected to get married. From the time you are born you know you are a girl and so you're expected to get married and have babies. Sometimes I think there are other things I want to do. But it's hard to know where to start. It's like your world has sides on it, big walls that are very high and stop you getting out and moving in other worlds. I want to get my head together properly or else it is going to mean that my daughter will just grow up and feel the same way I do. She'll get trapped too.

Anita, housewife

Big ball of anger

Sometimes, you know, I'm just damned tired. There have been many times when I have felt that if this is all there is, then I'm not sure it is worth it. I get up very early every morning and so does my husband. We have to. He has to drive a long way to his construction site and I have to make the children's lunches, then take the baby over to the sitter's place. I start work at 8 o'clock. I get home by about 5:30, just a bit before my husband. We're both exhausted by then. But he starts to watch television. I start to get dinner and try to help the kids where I can with their work. After, there are always piles of washing and ironing. When we go to bed, he wants to make love. By then I don't want to even move any more.

I'm angry. Sometimes I think I am angry all the time. And this anger goes into my bones and my muscles and my hair and my teeth. Sometimes I don't feel like anything more than one big ball of anger. And he wants me to make love.

Laura, production assembler

Family honour

When I was 24, my boyfriend and I decided that I would try to get pregnant so that my parents would have to agree to our getting married. Before that, they wouldn't even consider it. My family is Sicilian and I've got an older sister who is 25 and who is still not married. They wouldn't hear of my getting married before her. So it was the only way. They didn't like it, and my mother beat me up. But finally, they had to let us, to save the honour of the family.

Rosa, secretary

Iron it all out

So I feel inferior. That's what I have to end up admittin' to myself.
I start off in Jamaica and it's not so bad. I got this good job with the
government and things are not so bad. So my ol' lady there she
decides to up and better herself. She comes to Canada. I think it's a
good thing. She never had an education. She's got no idea about
anythin'. So she comes and starts to get fancy ideas here. Now she
goes to school and does a bit of work in her spare time.

I come too, but I only get a job in a steel foundry. It's not so bad.
I get just over $5 an hour. But I'm workin' all the time. She's fillin'
up her head. Says she's goin' be a this or she's goin' be a that. Okay,
so I get mad sometimes. "Let's talk," she says. "Let's talk and sort
out how we feel." I don' know what's happened to her. She's not
the same any more and I'm slavin' my bloody life out in the foundry. Just another black immigrant. Nowhere to go here. But she fig-
ures we ought to talk and iron it all out. I'm just a black immigrant
here and that means inferior. Do you know what I mean?

Harry, steel foundry worker

22 Neither here nor there

You want the very best for your children. But the culture, the values seem different here. Sometimes you feel you must resist. And your children are caught between two worlds.

It's a sin

I'm 18 years old and I can't do anything. I can't go out. If I do I have to lie about it. I have to be home around 7:00 or 7:30, and that's it. I'm not enjoying life. My parents just don't understand what it is to be with a guy or with friends. That you don't have to do anything wrong.

They believe that the guys are supposed to come to you. They're supposed to knock on the door and say, "You've got two daughters. Who's married and who's not?" They don't believe in going out on dates or dancing or going to social gatherings. They don't believe in that at all. I can do anything during the daytime up until 7 o'clock or 8 o'clock when the action really starts. Then I have to stay home. And that's why many times my parents and I have arguments.

We went to Huntsville on a school trip and my Dad started teasing me and saying, "I still have to find out where you went. I still have to find out who you were with. I still have to find out who your friends are." He really got me upset. So I said to him, "Look Dad, I can't take it any more. If this goes on I'm going to run away from home and I'm not coming back." He didn't answer me. I was really surprised. He usually says to me that whatever he says is for my own good. But I told him that I didn't believe this was true, that I respected his ideas but he couldn't expect me to live by them. And I think I'm going to try him out. One day, if I really want to go somewhere with someone, whether it's a boy or a girl, I'm just going to go. Hopefully, I'll come back and find the door open. But it's a chance I'll have to take.

It's hard to have dates. Nobody asks you. Because of my background, because I'm Portuguese, guys tend to not look at me. They talk to me all right, but they don't get personal. They seem to think, "Oh, she's Portuguese. She won't be able to go out on dates."

My parents are always telling me that everything I do is a sin. If I talk bad, it's a sin. If I answer back, it's a sin. If I come in late, it's a sin. It's a sin. It's a sin.

It's hard to be a girl when your parents are not Canadian. People on TV do everything that your parents don't.

Natalie, high school student

Virgin

I have a cousin about the same age as me. He takes out Canadian girls. He's really cute. He has about six or seven girls that he fools around with. But he says, "When I get married, I'm going to marry a Portuguese girl, because she'll be sure to be a virgin and she'll stay home all the time." One day when he said that to me I slapped him right across the face.

Teresa, high school student

A little bit of sunshine

I been in Canada since I was eight years old, so sure, I'm Canadian. And what's that mean to me? I dunno. I mean – well – to be a Canadian, that means you've got a passport that says "Canada" and you can go all over the world and they got to let you in 'cause you're Canadian. Right?

My life hasn't changed too much since I been here. At least, I don't remember too much what it was like before. I was small and I don't think you specially consider what things are like when you're small. That's just how things are. And you change it anyway.

I really like it here. We got all the things we need. . . . I suppose there is just one thing I could say about being a Canadian who wasn't exactly born here. It means you got all the benefits of being a Canadian but you always seem to be a bit on the outside. You're not quite the same as other people. Even if you try hard to be like them.

My mama and papa are not like other parents of my friends. They speak pretty good English, not too much of an accent or anything. Especially my father. My mother gets a bit mixed up with the English grammar sometimes. But my father speaks perfect English. But it's not how he speaks, it's what he says and the way he looks. My father is a man who likes to talk. Everywhere he goes he starts to talk to people. Not stupid things that don't make sense. Just friendly. And he laughs a lot. Mama laughs too. She doesn't talk too much, but she laughs. And people don't always appreciate it. Like most people on a bus here, don't just start to talk to their neighbour. But my papa sits right down and starts to say something friendly.

He talks a lot about the sun. Like, "Hey, what's happening to that sun that's shining way up there somewhere. We need sun to live, don't we?" And then he laughs. But you'd be amazed how many people just look at him like he's crazy. And they try to move away from him, so he won't bother them any more. But Papa doesn't really try to bother anyone. If they would know him they would know he just wants to be friendly. That's the Mexican way, he tells me. "A little bit of sunshine wherever you go. You can't go wrong that way." He's always saying that. I wonder sometimes if he really believes it. I never seen him get angry when people look at him strangely. Not even once. He just sort of smiles and then kind of nods to himself.

When I was little, I remember how much fun it always was with Papa. If I was somewhere there was a staircase, I could always slide down. He'd lift me up and hold me up all the way down. With him you always do things the fun way. But now – since I been about 11

– I get a bit embarrassed sometimes. It's hard to always be so different from other people.

My father is a good man, and I think that sometimes maybe it's been a bit hard for him living here. Just in the last couple of years I been starting to notice things. I don't know if he didn't have a steady job some of the time or if he was just laid off a while. When you're a kid you don't pay too much attention to those things. But just lately, I started remembering back to lots of different times. Papa has had many different jobs. One time he worked at a place that made locks. Another time he used to load trains. Then sometimes, even now, he goes off to work on farms. But we always stay here, Mama and the boys and me. Because Papa says that school is the big number one.

I do pretty good at school. Some of my teachers I really like a lot. Sometimes they aren't too fair, though. Like once, when it was my first Easter in Canada. We had a play at school and it was about the life of Jesus from when he was born to the Crucifixion. This teacher said that whoever was quietest in the class would be picked for a part. I didn't speak one word. All the other kids were whispering and making a lot of noise. I wouldn't allow myself to open my mouth. Even when we were singing a hymn and one of the boys started making his voice go funny like a tuba. Everyone was laughing. I made myself stare at a spot at the back of the room and just not laugh. I wanted so badly to be picked. And then this teacher came by and she nearly picked me and this nun who was with her said, "Can you imagine an angel that colour?" It made me feel strange.

Felicia, 14 years old

No one to kiss them

I worry about the children. They have no one to kiss them and hug them and touch them. We are like that in Italy. We show our love like that. Here, nobody touches you. It is all different.

Tina, housewife

Church

I had a will to make something of our lives here. But later when I used to see my eldest son sitting in the corner without any friends or anything to do, his eyes just dead, as we say, that hurt me very much. It was what kept me alive. To be everything for the children.

The boys picked up English fairly fast. We belonged to a congregation of the Christian Reform Church in Kitchener. Once in a while, we could go in to church. Not too much because we had no car and it was 23 miles from Kitchener. So I remember that when we did get a car our family was too big to go with one car. One day half of the family would go to church, and the next week the other half. With the older children we kept speaking Dutch at home but I had to learn English from the children. You know, you have to keep knowing what they are thinking. They can't say anything to me if I don't know what they are saying.

Clazien, housewife

Embarrassed

In the summer here lots of kids wear halters and culottes and sensible, cool clothes like that to school. But when I want to dress like that my parents have a fit. "Girls in Latin America don't go to school like that," they say. "Girls in our country show respect for their teachers," they tell me. I got so fed up with the girls in Latin America. I am Canadian now and I want to be like the others. Anyway, my parents are still thinking of Uruguay 10 years ago. I bet it's all changed now.

The big problem for my parents is that they are neither there nor here. The country they remember there must have changed since they've been gone, but they have never really got used to being in Canada either. They don't belong anywhere any more.

I got this part in a school play. I had to play this girl who was – well – she was sort of a bad girl, if you know what I mean. When my father heard about it he made me drop out of the play. "No daughter of mine is going to go off with any boy to sleep – not on the stage, not on the street," he yelled at me. That time, I wasn't only mad, I was really embarrassed. I thought a lot about that. It made me feel very different from the other kids.

Lilia, 17 years old

Fooling around

The pure Canadian people are the Indian people. The rest of us are all foreigners. So they can't accuse me for coming to this country. They came maybe ahead of me, but way back they were one of the same kind of people.

I'm happy my kids are going to grow up in Canada. I wouldn't dream of taking them back and letting them live in Lebanon. In any shape or form that you want to look at it, I think Canada is the best country in the world. But there is one thing – the way they bring up their children here is a different way than we do ourselves. I'd like to bring up my children the same way they're bringing up their children, but there is something different in between. I wouldn't allow my daughter to go on the street and live by herself when she's only 14 years old. I would rather keep them under control until they are mature enough to get married. Then they will go on their own.

I know my daughters will be mixing with the Canadian people. But still, in our home we keep training them and keep talking to them. We keep teaching them to be like Lebanese girls. Here in Canada if a girl is 16 years old and she doesn't have a boyfriend, the rest of the kids start laughing at her. There must be something wrong with you. But for us, a girl can have her friends, she can go out, but up to a certain point. After she's been out for so many hours she has to be back home. And she has to know exactly what she's doing.

It's different for a boy. A boy always has the authority to do what he wants. A boy takes responsibility no matter how young he is. Girls are weak. You have to keep after them. You have to keep teaching them, giving them all your love and your idea of life all the time, before they get themselves in a mess. While the boys can understand you when they're 10 or 15 years old, the girls they don't.

When my daughters start growing up a little and they know their way to school and then back home, they will get the same routine all the time. If they are late, they will get a punishment. And from the first time when you give them a good punishment they wouldn't do it any more. They'll know they have a father and mother waiting home for them, so they have to come back home. And we can teach them and give them all the lessons they want so that they know what to expect if they stay late. We will teach them as much as we can just to keep them out of trouble. We want to live the Canadian life and at the same time the value of our family has to be there. If my daughter wants to fool around on the street, I don't know what I'll do.

Harry, baker

Canadian

I'm the best hockey player in the world, so I must be Canadian now.

Mark, four years old

23 A mirror for the soul

All the known things have disappeared. The familiar landmarks are gone now. Friends are hard to find; families are often far away. On the streets, in the buses and trains, people are strangers. Or is it you that is the stranger?

Gaiety

I am a very gay person. I love to sing and dance. But people here are not usually like that and slowly I find all that gaiety being squeezed out of me. Sometimes, I find that I'm beginning to feel like all the people I see on the streets and the buses here – without any joy or gaiety at all. And that really frightens me.

Mary, executive secretary

Something is left empty

As an immigrant, I'm not sure that my life is interesting to other people. I have travelled a great deal in Scandinavia, France and Holland and I have worked all over the place. I speak a number of languages. It is easy for us to do that in Europe. We are all so close together and we can travel easily. We go from one place to the other because the distances are not like in Canada, so vast. I have done many jobs working for film companies, publishing houses and in television. Coming here to Canada was not hard. I am used to being on my own and meeting new people. I have found that if you are friendly to people they respond to you.

Now I think I am beginning to feel a little bit Canadian. I will stay here to live. It is a good life. I am not too interested in material things but it is a satisfying feeling to have a job you like to do and an attractive apartment, plus the possibility of taking vacations all over the world.

Perhaps there is one thing I have learned as a traveller, a woman traveller. Sure, I get lonely sometimes. I used to get very lonely when I first came to Canada and didn't know anyone. Then, sure, I want to be with an attractive man. It is not really difficult. I have found that a man very seldom refuses an involvement with a young, attractive woman if she shows an interest in him. As far as she wants to go, he will go. And it doesn't matter if he is married. He seems always to be able to justify it. Sometimes, I wonder how they lie to their wives or maybe to themselves. Sometimes I wonder what would happen if their wives walked in and saw us together.

Perhaps I make it sound sordid. Please, I don't know if you understand me. I am not a promiscuous person, but yes, I have had involvements with men. Most of them have been pleasant encounters, exciting. It is easy to be excited with someone you know just a little bit. You can convince each other you understand the other person perfectly. But even when I have enjoyed these encounters and have become quite sentimentally involved, something inside me is left empty. I keep thinking if he is like this with me now, he would be like this with someone else after a while. Men, even attractive, intelligent men who have achieved something, are like starved little boys. They have great egos. And it is the same here as in Europe.

I would like to meet the married man who would refuse an involvement with me because of his commitment to his woman. Maybe it's just as well I don't meet that kind of man. I think if I ever met a man with that kind of integrity I would love him very much. That would be ironic, eh?

Ingrid, private secretary

Loneliness

Loneliness is one of the biggest problems for single women. You feel very isolated. And from what I have seen it is just as difficult for many Canadian women to make friends as it is for any immigrant.

Of course, the immigrant woman has the added problem that she doesn't speak the language. But the average young Canadian, living away from home, who works in an office or who teaches school doesn't have many friends either and she tries to find affection wherever she can.

I remember once when I got together with some Canadian girls and, as it is not difficult to get drugs here, they were smoking marijuana. I don't know if it was from the effect of the drugs or just from sheer loneliness, but two of them started to kiss and embrace each other. The situation was difficult for me. This particular night I had invited a young Spanish friend, considerably younger than the rest of us, she was only 20 years of age. I felt very uncomfortable, perhaps not so much for myself as for her. The others wanted me to get involved with them but I reacted by keeping absolutely out of the whole business.

I have often asked myself since why I didn't become involved that night. Was it because I hadn't been smoking. (The truth is I never smoke and I didn't smoke that night either.) Was it that the other Spanish girl was there and I felt protective or even ashamed? Or was it that I just am not attracted sexually to women, not even under circumstances where it seems acceptable? There is no doubt that my education socialized me very strongly away from this.

Afterwards I spoke at length to one of the women and saw that her loneliness, her need to have someone, was as great as my own. I believe it's a terrible problem we all have to solve, but that night it seemed to me they were trying to find a solution to this in each other.

Vicky, language teacher

Alone

When I would have my time off I would walk around the streets. I know all the streets of Montreal. Every one. It was better to walk around than to be alone in my room. My brother had five children. He was busy. He did not want me.

For years I worked, and on weekends I walked the streets. Then I got sick. It was a nervous breakdown. I was frightened. I was crazy, in a crazy-house. I had heard of such places. There were many women there from Germany, Portugal, Greece – from all places and mainly women, even born here. Young ones of 18 and 20. The doctor came but we could not understand what the other one was saying. But I was lucky. Downstairs in the cafeteria was a Polish woman working in the kitchen. When the doctor came I would go quickly downstairs and bring her up to my room and she told him what I was saying.

After six weeks I went out of hospital to my brother's house. For nearly a year I lived there. But then he said I must go on my own. It is not nice to go home always to be alone. I do not want to be alone any more.

Joan, unemployed

My best friend

It was lonely in the beginning when I couldn't talk to people. My first friend here, she is still my best friend, is a Canadian, a Métis. She came one day to my house. I just found this lady sitting on my steps outside the door. I was wondering what she wanted. I was a big chicken, I didn't even dare go out. But she wouldn't go away. Finally, I just had to go to see what she wanted. She said that our children were already playing together and she thought she would like to meet me. I invited her in and made her a cup of tea. She was talking quite a bit, and I was mostly listening. But slowly it got better.

Wilma, housewife

Talking

I remember once a few years ago, another immigrant woman came to me with some awful problem with Unemployment Insurance. They wouldn't pay her, and even after weeks went by, they still wouldn't pay. I had spoken to her a few times before, but I decided to try to resolve the problem for her. I went to the UIC office with her. We took the streetcar and spent about 45 minutes together on the journey. After a while, she started telling me about when she had come to Canada and why. She told me all about her relationship with her husband. It was like a nightmare. She wouldn't stop talking.

She came from what she considered a very good family and the husband didn't. And she was trying very hard to maintain their dignity amongst all the chaos of their lives. They had problems with the kids, the kids were sick, the husband was making very little money, she was working as a cleaner at night. Her whole concept of her life and her family had been upset and she was trying to cope with all this in the best way she could. But the fact that there was so little money meant that the differences between her and her husband became even more acute. She went on and on and on and on and on. She so desperately needed someone to talk to. She had very few friends, and she wouldn't meet her husband's friends because they weren't quite up to her standards. So she was extremely isolated. She was very close to a nervous breakdown. She talked without stopping. Talking and talking just to be able to say things she had never said before. I'll never forget her. I was just like a mirror for her own soul. And there are so many like her.

Fernanda, human rights worker

Servant

My school years were like a bit of fantasy. Nothing was ever what it seemed to be. The first day, the very first day at school I didn't have a clue. No way I could understand what was going on. I remember playing house or something like that with three other girls in my class. I can't remember exactly what we were doing. I just recall a part of the school ground where you could get partly under a building. It wasn't very high and we had to bend down all the time. But

173

it was sort of private and I got the idea that it was special for me to be there with them. I think they probably only asked me to play with them because they could make me do what they wanted.

Anyway, I remember very clearly we had bits of coloured glass that we pretended were plates and things. They had these things stashed away there. I was the servant in the family. At least I got that impression, and I was very worried that I would not do the right things because I couldn't really understand anything they were saying and one of the girls terrified me because she was very fat and quite bossy. Anyway, I dropped some of the little pieces of glass and then she, the fat one, started to scold me. I was very frightened. I could tell she was angry and I didn't know if it was real or just in the game. I ran away from there crying and crying. One of the teachers found me and was really worried about what had happened to me. But I couldn't tell them anything. I wasn't even sure what they were saying to me.

It was like that in one way or another all through my school years. Most of the kids were French-Canadians and even the other immigrant kids were from Greece or Italy or somewhere like that. To me, they might just as well have been French. There was a Japanese boy a couple of grades higher than me. All the kids used to take me to him when I couldn't understand them. They seemed to think we were both the same. But he didn't understand my Chinese and it just made me feel worse.

I learned French pretty fast, and then as a teenager I spent a couple of years in Sudbury with my brother's family and there I learned English. But at home all through my growing up years we always spoke Chinese. It always made home and school two quite separate things for me. For instance, I always thought all the other kids were millionaire's kids. I don't know why. Maybe it was because I had heard that everyone in America was rich and I really didn't know too much about the lives of any of the other kids in my class.

I remember one day one of the girls in my class had a birthday party and her mother and father took all of the class to a restaurant for coke and hamburgers. There were about, I don't know, maybe 25 of us, maybe only 20. Anyway, I remember when her father opened up his wallet to pay the bill, I saw lots and lots of money there. I nearly fainted. I couldn't take my eyes off him. I thought he was real, real rich. I thought things like that for a long time. It made everything unreal for me because I would build up an idea about something and then one day I'd learn it was really different to what I thought. And then I'd have to rearrange everything in my mind.

I never really worried about work or what I'd be. My brother has a restaurant. Y'know a Chinese restaurant. Chinese and Canadian it is. Anyway, he took over when my dad retired. My dad's quite old now. So I work in the restaurant. And it's not too bad. Sometimes I think it might be easier to work in a place that your family didn't own, 'cause my brother's real hard to please. Real, real hard. But I guess it's not too bad. And like, my family is quite close and they expect you to more or less stay together, so I never really thought of any other kind of job.

Eloise, waitress

I lost my own language

Never, never again would I come to a place where I didn't speak one word of English. What it does to you is hard to tell. Even now to look back, say how things were, doesn't seem too bad. But I remember the cost to me inside.

My very first job when I came here was on an extra gang, working on the railroad. We used to go out, 10 or 12 of us in a gang, and check the lines. We lived in a railroad car and every couple of weeks they'd take us back for a weekend in town. I didn't have much money. We only earned about 85 cents an hour, though we could do lots of overtime. Saturdays and Sundays you could work 14 or

15 hours a day. But I was a single guy and I didn't want to spend my time sitting at home looking at myself. So on the weekends, I'd go to the local dance.

It was pretty bad, I tell you. I didn't speak one word of English and often the girls wouldn't dance with me. But it wasn't like at home in Rumania. There if they said "no" to one fellow, they'd have to sit the dance out. Here, they'd say "no" to you when you asked them and then get up with the next fellow who asked them. Boy, did that make me feel bad. I thought there was something wrong with me. It really bothered me. But after a while, the other fellows I worked with said I shouldn't let it get me down, because they did it to everyone. It wasn't only me. But you know, those things really worry you when you come to a new place. No language. No friends.

I did that work on the gang for about two and a half years. After that, I told them I would only go out with a gang that spoke English. No German or Ukrainian fellows. I knew I had to learn English somehow. Then I got a job as a hospital orderly. It wasn't much money but it was an inside job. Steady. I got married then to a Canadian girl. We got two sons now.

You know, I hardly even speak my own language any more. There's one old fellow I know, but he's the only one I speak with any more. It's funny. I wanted to learn English and in doing that I lost my own language.

George, hospital orderly

Rejected

When my baby was about six months, I got a job as a sewing machine operator in a factory. I earned 67 cents an hour. I had to leave the baby with my older daughter who was seven years old. My husband had a job but. . . .

I started to look for a better job, always as a sewing machine operator. My husband found a better job, too, as a carpenter. We got our house and our life started to be much happier. Our Ukrainian community here was very strong and we belonged to the choir, to the theatre, to other activities, just so that we might forget about our daily life.

I kept working, but only part-time, between children and sickness and whatever else came up. First I was a sewing machine operator night shift, cleaning woman day shift, then I got a job as a Ukrainian language teacher. It was poorly paid but I loved it.

Sometimes I felt rejected by the Canadian society, but I continued to be active in our own community as it developed culturally over the years. We have a very rich culture and folklore and we wanted our children to learn to know and love it, too.

Natalia, teacher's aide

I had to go

It's okay now. I just go to school now like the other kids. Some of them don't be nice to me. If they're mean to me, I don't like them either. I go to two schools. As well as the ordinary English school I go to Greek school twice a week. But school here is much easier than in Cyprus. There, they gave us much more work. Here, it's so easy. There's a Greek Sunday school here for us, too. The priest says it in Greek chapel and then you go downstairs to the hall and we have different ladies and they explain it in English for the children who can't understand it in Greek.

When we first got here my father used to listen to the radio all the time. When he had to go to work, he'd make my mother listen for him. He was so worried all the time. After a while he got sick and had to go to the doctor. My mother used to cry a lot then. Every time when I'd come home from school, she'd be putting my lunch on the table and she'd by crying and crying.

At the first school I went to they were beating me up all the time. I don't know why. I wasn't doing nothing. I guess they just didn't like me. I would try to run away. Sometimes I would cry if they really beat me a lot. But sometimes I didn't cry. Then we moved and I had to go to a different school. My teacher she said, "Why are you leaving? 'Cause the kids are beating you up?" But I said "no." It isn't nice to tell your teacher that the kids in her own class are so bad.

I had this friend and she liked me a lot. Then this other girl she didn't like me and she told this other girl not to play with me. And so she never played with me anymore. They used to call me names and say I was Greek. After a while I just went home. But I didn't feel so good.

The children in my country didn't want me to go. They liked me so much. But I had to. My country is nice. It is all sunshine. One day, I would like to go back.

Maria, eight years old

Friends

For me, one of the most painful things is that I left my friends. I have my immediate family, and that's it. I think now I'll die without friends here.

Erica, lab technician

VI

THE COUNTRY
AND THE
PEOPLE

24 Alone in an enemy camp

You have arrived, a stranger in a strange land. Sometimes it is hard to know what people think of you, but sometimes it is all too obvious. How much of yourself must you give up to belong here? Can you ever really be accepted by other Canadians?

Summer weekends

When I first came here, I was working in a small dress shop where the boss was Jewish. I did alterations. I also made the coffee, cleaned the floor and did a lot of other jobs. But I liked it. I only earned $80 a week but it was easy work for me. Sometimes the hours were very long but, if you can believe it, I was happy with my $80 a week.

After I had been there for about four months, my boss asked me would I like to go with his family to their cottage up at the lake for the weekend. I didn't know anything more of Canada than downtown Montreal, so I was happy to go. They picked me up at my uncle's house on Saturday and we drove for about two and a half hours into the country.

The house at the lake was very big and comfortable. There were a lot of people there, all friends of my boss and his wife. When we arrived they started to have drinks and some went swimming. I helped to prepare lunch, then afterwards I washed the dishes and the boss's wife showed me what vegetables to start to prepare for dinner. I worked in their kitchen for the whole weekend. Not once did I even have a swim and I could not talk too much to anyone. Nobody spoke Portuguese and nobody was interested in the few words of English I was able to use. So that although my meals were all provided and there were even a few hours when I was free with nothing to do, I was all alone and not sure what I should do. We stayed there until Monday night and then they drove me home again and dropped me at my uncle's house.

I was a bit foolish, I suppose. My uncle had not wanted me to go up to the cottage with them. He doubted their motives, though I am not certain what he thought they wanted me for. But we had had a big argument before I went, so I told everyone that it had been very nice, that the people had been friendly and I had been swimming all the time, and things like that.

Because of my stupid lying to them, I went up again the next weekend when my boss and his wife asked me. And then for a couple of months I kept going. But it was always the same – a lot of people and a lot of work for me, cooking, washing dishes, setting the table. After a while, I didn't want to go any more and I told my boss. He became angry and said I would lose my job if I didn't go. I went for two weekends more. But then it was unpleasant at the shop because I was angry and the boss was threatening me all the time. I still did not want to explain it to my uncle. I thought he would laugh at me and make fun of my foolishness, and I knew he would be angry, too.

I tried to get another job because every day it was worse at the shop. I hated it now. I felt like a prisoner. I went to two other shops looking for jobs but they must have been friends of my boss. He knew that I had been looking for another job and he fired me. I was so shocked that it could happen like that and so afraid of what my uncle would say if he knew I would not be bringing in any money that for four days I left the house at the normal time to go to work and came home as usual around eight at night. I didn't say that I was just walking up and down streets looking for another job.

Finally, I found work in a big factory where I get the same money. But the work is very hard. I don't make anything now. I just sew up pieces, the same pieces, day after day. Before at least, I could move around a bit when I was tired of being at the machine. Now I must stay there until it is time for a break or lunch. The factory is big and the building is very cold. I have never told my uncle the real reason why I left the other place. Sometimes, I even wish I had stayed there. But I used to feel they owned me. That I was like a slave to the boss and his wife. I am learning that there are many ways to be a slave.

Jacinta, sewing machine operator

The colour of your skin

When you first realize you are not getting a fair chance because of your colour, it makes you depressed. You don't want to talk to anyone. Slowly you get very thick-skinned, then you become pushy. If anyone says anything to me about my colour, I can give an answer right back to them. My children don't agree with me about colour discrimination here. They say there is none. But they are young and attractive, and they have had their schooling here.

I remember when my son first started school here. He was 10. He really suffered. He didn't want his father to go to school to pick him up. The other children would tease him because his father had a turban and a brown skin. He said they teased him, too, about his skin and he would just give them a left and a right. But when they said it about his father he felt very bad. The colour of your skin really makes a big difference here. A very big difference.

Kamla, unemployed

Integration

The trouble with a lot of immigrants is that they seem to think it possible to have a dream world where they can become, more or less, Canadian, but where they can retain the best parts of their old life, too. That would be beautiful if it were possible, but it's not. I know, because I tried it.

I met my husband in my own country. We hardly had a language in common but we liked each other immediately and enjoyed being together. We fell in love and within three months we were married. In the beginning, our different cultures were no drawback. I was learning English as quickly as I could, and as he was in my country, everything was new and different to him.

We came to Windsor right after we were married. Culture differences didn't matter too much in the first few months. I was pregnant, living in a suburb, trying to cope with shopping in a plaza and being able to speak to my neighbours. I became Canadianized very quickly, but when the baby was born I suffered a kind of a reaction. I wanted her to have a Polish name. I wanted to meet people who spoke Polish. I wanted to speak to her in Polish. I was suffering from delayed culture shock.

My husband was very resentful. He seemed to feel it was a rejection of him. There was no way he would agree to the baby having a "foreign" name. No way he felt I should talk Polish with anyone in front of him, as he did not understand it. In fact, he made it very clear that he did not want a "foreign" wife. I was alone in the enemy camp and I very quickly surrendered.

Perhaps he was right, or perhaps I had been wrong in the beginning to be so ready to change who and what I was. In any case, for anyone concerned with the complete integration of an immigrant, the way I did it was the very best way. Integration equals annihilation.

Mari, housewife

A kind of arrogance

I guess it really isn't quite the same for immigrants from the British Isles. We don't have nearly as many problems as other people who come here not knowing the language or anything about the culture. There is a kind of arrogance, too, that probably keeps us going. A personal story I can tell you reflects this and really is a bit of a put-down of us, too.

When my husband and I came to Canada it was just at the end of the war. We sailed to New York on a troop ship. As we got close to port, we were up on deck with all the other passengers. Suddenly over the loudspeaker a voice said, "All foreigners please proceed to Stateroom B for immigration clearance."

We sat there for a while longer and then asked an officer where we should go. "You heard the announcement," he said. "All foreigners to Stateroom B."

"But we're British," we blurted out. Immediately, of course, we realized our mistake. It just had never occurred to us we would be considered foreigners.

Betty, housewife

Epilepsy

If I go back 21 years to when I came here first, everything was different — language, the farm, the food. The one constant thing was religion.

We love our children. They are the first thing that you have when you come here that is your own. Sometimes though, the children of immigrants suffer a great deal. My second son was born quite normal. But after a few years, he started to get sick once in a while. One day we were visiting Dutch friends and he just "went." I saw many things in the war and I thought he was having a convulsion. But it turned out to be a mild form of epilepsy. With the help of a Dutch doctor we went back through his school records and found that so much pressure was put on him throughout the years that he started to buckle under the strain. He was slapped and blamed for everything. His teacher discriminated always against this little Dutch boy.

It is the older people who discriminate. They are the ones that are afraid to see their world change, to see new things happen. The young people are concerned about each other. They are more prepared to take things and people as they come. And that's what we all have to do. Start to accept people as they are whatever the colour of their skin.

Riet, farm woman

Wop

I want to be a cop. Everyone has got all these reasons why I shouldn't. First of all they say, "Do you ever see any Italian cops around?" That really bothers me. It really makes me want to do it. Then they say I'm only five-foot-two. But I bet there are a lot of male cops shorter than I am. And then they think that just because I'm a woman I couldn't handle the situation of being a cop. When I told my mom, she didn't like the idea at all. She wants me to sit in front of a typewriter. But there's no way I'm going to do that. But now I've begun to think about it twice. Say I get married. Who has ever seen a short, Italian, female, pregnant cop?

I've got a boyfriend right now. He's Canadian. My mom knows but not my dad. It doesn't trouble her so much that he's Canadian. Just that he's a guy. And if we're going out now, that means that within a year or so we have to get married. But how am I supposed to know if I like the guy enough to get married to him?

Sometimes he calls me a "wop," or he jokes with me about pizza. It seems like the Italians invented the pizza. Then he comes up with the fact that it wasn't the Italians at all. Sometimes I feel bad when he does this. Why does he have to keep on about the fact that I am Italian. But I'm not quite sure how he means it. I don't know. Maybe I take it too harshly. Maybe I'm too serious about it. But it hurts me. I wish he wouldn't do it.

Carmela, high school student

Greeks, not pigs

"They don't seem to be able to do too good in New York, so how do they expect me to be able to handle my own little United Nations in this place?" That's what the foreman said one day when he came around where we were eating lunch and all talking Greek. Of the 14 of us that work there, eight are Greek and one of the Italians speaks Greek, too. That's one of the things I feel the Canadian foreman doesn't like. That we speak Greek and he doesn't know what we are saying. I won't say we never talk about him, but at least it isn't necessary for him to know what we say about him. Often when he speaks to us in English, it is very important that we understand him, and very difficult for us too. He should think about that sometimes. One day I'm going to ask him if he thinks that just because we do not speak good English we do not need clean washrooms and a proper place to eat our lunch. We are Greeks, not pigs.

Margarita, factory worker

Englishmen need not apply

There is a certain bigotry here, a bias that seems to be dormant and only comes to the surface when there are economic problems — high unemployment like we're going through now, or whatever. At the beginning of the Second World War, there were factories in Toronto that posted notices offering employment stating: Englishmen need not apply.

Jim, plumber

Bananas

My mum brought me up to date Chinese boys, to only look at Chinese boys. If I were to marry another colour, she'd disown me.

I was sitting on the porch with my grandmother and this Chinese girl went by with a black guy. My grandmother looked at me and said, "Look at that!" I didn't react at all. As a matter of fact I wear glasses and I didn't have them on. I couldn't see anything. So she went on, "Look at that, she's out with a black boy. If I ever see you doing anything like that I'll kill you."

And it's not only your family. If some Hong Kong guy sees a Chinese girl going out with a white guy he will walk by her and say in Chinese, "Are all the Chinese guys dead?" The guys that come from Hong Kong call us bananas. They say we're yellow on the outside and white on the inside.

Glenna, high school student

Making faces

At the beginning of the year, some of the English Canadian parents always make faces when they see I am their children's teacher. Sometimes, of course, if these children are slow learners their parents would like to blame me. But I don't mind this any more. I see it as a challenge. And, if I say so myself, I think I produce one of the best grade one classes in the school because I treat all the children equally and do not discriminate against them if they do not speak the language.

Lolita, teacher

Paki

I was six when we first came here. I don't remember much that we had problems. I suppose we did. It seems to me that to be a Pakistani in Canada is the biggest problem of all. We got a place to live over a bakery and we just stayed there. It's pretty big and there's room for our family. My father, he got a job as an accountant, so he was happy. Elementary school was all right. Junior high was at the same place and I knew all the kids. I used to like school. I didn't seem to be any different from anyone else. But when I hit senior high school everything changed for me. It was as if I had just arrived in the country. I went into a school where there were quite a few ethnic kids, but only three or four, maybe a few more, East Indians. I think there were only two Pakistanis in the whole school.

It was hard to make friends in the school. "Rag-head" and "Paki" – all those things they started to call me. Some of them were really stupid. I don't wear a turban, but maybe they were too dumb to notice it. One day I came out of school and the tires on my bike were slashed. It happened about six times. I stopped taking my bike to school. No one ever saw anyone doing anything in that school. Not if they did it to a Paki. I only told one teacher about it. He was my science teacher. A really great man. He kicked up some fuss with the principal, but no one did anything. At one assembly the principal asked whoever did it to come to his office. Naturally, no one came. But one morning, that science teacher told me his tires on his car were slashed during the night. It made me feel pretty bad.

I quit school that year, at the end of grade 11. My Dad was so mad about that he never spoke to me for four months. I never really explained at home why I was quitting. It wouldn't do any good. My father is the sort of immigrant who feels every bit of discrimination has to be fought. Maybe he is right. But I don't think it makes any difference. I knew that if we really made a big fuss about it, the school might go along for a bit, more or less because they had to. But it wouldn't help me with the other kids.

After a while you get used to not having friends. Most of the fellows that seemed friendly, even they dropped off being friends after a while, because they started to get it too. You go around with a "Paki" makes you just as bad.

I got a job in a pharmacy now. The man where I work is very fair to me. He is encouraging me to go to night school. He says I could become a pharmacist. But I don't want to become a pharmacist. I want to be a doctor.

Ali, 16 years old

Take your clothes off

The minute you say you are a Doukhobour, people look at you and expect you to take your clothes off.

Katherine, youth organizer

Working guest

It was my destiny always to be alone in the crucial moments of my married life. I came to Canada alone with my two young sons. My husband stayed in Egypt to finish off the business. The only address that I had when we arrived was of a young woman whose parents I had known in Egypt. She was married to an ex-serviceman who was back at university studying. They had bought a house and she had just given birth to twins. So when I appeared on the scene, I was a godsend to them.

I phoned from Montreal to say that it was so cold that our nostrils were freezing together. The children and I used to walk once around the block and then we would have to go inside because it was so intensely cold for us. This young woman told me on the phone that it was not nearly so cold in Toronto and that we should come down right away. So we came and moved into their basement apartment. At the time, they knew nothing of me but my name and the fact that I had come from Egypt. I think that if they had known I was Jewish they would not have invited me to move in with them. The house was in the fashionable Kingsway area and, at least in those days, it was definitely a restricted area.

It was 1951 and I had some trouble getting my 12-year-old son into the Etobicoke school system. The gentleman in whose house we lived went with him to register him to prove that he had a right to go to the local school because he lived in the area. I have no proof that it was because he was Jewish that there were difficulties. I have never allowed myself to believe in such discrimination unless it is thrown in my face. However, there is always a nagging suspicion.

When my husband came and joined us, we had to move from these surroundings because he felt it degrading that I was, more or less, the servant in the house. I didn't mind. I was both a paying guest and a working guest, but I was quite happy.

Hedy, retired

189

Turn out the lights

When my husband and I wanted to get married, it caused a minor revolution. Not even so minor. His parents threatened him with everything if he married a black girl. We knew it would be hard for them to accept. We'd talked about it a lot ourselves. We even wondered for a few months before we finally decided if we really ought to get married. When he first told them, his mother became ill and they thought she might have been having a heart attack. They had only met me once at that stage and had been very cool to me. And while she was ill I didn't go anywhere near the house.

But after a couple of months, my parents asked them over. My own parents were not too happy about our plans either. They felt I should marry one of my own. It's funny they say that, though. Jim is just as much my own as anyone I've ever met, whatever their colour. Anyway, Jim had to do a lot of persuading, but his parents finally decided to come when they knew that my folks were not too happy either.

I've always known my mother was a very special lady, but that night she was superb. When Jim's parents had arrived and we were all sitting there together in the living room very uncomfortable and still and very formal, my mother in a quiet voice said, "If you'll excuse me, I'm going to turn out the light. I think that what we all need to talk about is best discussed if we are not sidetracked by colour." You know, after that, everyone started slowly to really talk about the problem. And how they felt. But really honestly. Nobody pretended any more. And after about three hours of sitting there in the dark bringing out all their fears, everyone seemed to feel okay. And they all decided they would not stand in our way, but would try to help us if the going got rough.

It hasn't been so rough, not really. We've got one baby and another one on the way. And there are two very devoted sets of grandparents.

Sari, housewife

190

DP

I'm a pretty even-tempered guy. I consider that you come to this country, you learn the language, you do a job and you mind your business. The only time I ever had a problem was when this guy called me a DP. Boy, did I want to punch him. I was ready to let him have it. Then this other Canadian guy he says to me it was no insult. DP means "displaced person." I calmed down when he explained it. But when I think about it, I still think that guy meant to insult me.

Oleg, railroad worker

Black like me

A lot of kids where I live don't want to play with me. They say if they're with me all the time they'll turn black, too.

Janey, grade three student

25 What does it mean to be Canadian?

The maple leaf. The beaver. The Rocky Mountains. The prairies. The lakes. The rivers. The snow. Images that will shape your new life. You look beyond them for the essence of the new land. You search hard for the place where you'll fit in.

This country hypnotized me

When I was a child I saw a movie about Canada called "The Valley of the Beavers." It was taken in the Rocky Mountains and the scenery was fabulous. At that time going to a movie was a real treat. Right then I decided that one day in my lifetime I would see the Rocky Mountains and that I would go on the Alaska Highway all the way to the Arctic Circle. That thought hung on to me, and when I arrived in Canada I did go right across the country from Montreal to Vancouver. I was so impressed. The country hypnotized me with its vastness. It did something to me.

I was raised on a small farm in France. I'd always been an outdoor type so when I got to B.C. I got a job in the forest industry. I had an agricultural school diploma from Europe. It included forestry also on a different scale, of course. But it was a big help to me. I worked in the central interior in very remote areas right up to the Yukon border. What an experience it was! But I had to learn English. I spoke only Dutch, German and French. I learnt on the job. Due to the vastness of the country I was always away from the towns. There was no night school where I was. I took some books with me and studied at nights. It took me three months to make myself understood. I worked in a group of about six or seven people. The amazing thing was that there were very few Canadians. I met people from Germany, Holland, Sweden, Spain, Norway – from all over – but very few Canadians.

My major tie here is the country itself. It attracts me in some strange way. However, coming from Europe I feel that I have gained a tremendous amount of experience that many Canadians have never had a chance to attain. It was a very different type of life in Europe when I left there. It was only 10 or 15 years after the war. We had suffered a lot in the war. We knew what hardship was. You don't forget that. And somehow, it prepares you a lot better for life. It doesn't matter what lies ahead of you, you are prepared.

I have a deep emotional attachment to the land here. Canada's big forests – to me, that's home. In 1971 was the B.C. Centennial. Many people made centennial projects of their own or on a group basis. Nobody asked me but I thought I'd do something. That year, the biggest snowmobile race in all of North America was to take place. A 200-mile trek on snowmobiles. I decided I would do the same trip myself under my own steam on snow-shoes, and beat the snowmobiles. I went to see the organizer and told him I was going to prove that a snowmobile is one thing but that you could accomplish a lot more on snowshoes. On snowshoes, you could go anywhere in the middle of the winter. He told me it was impossible. So I said that I would prove it to him. I would start nine days ahead of the snowmobilers and cover the same ground in the same time. But I'd start at the far end of the course and meet them at the starting line. We had to go over the mountains, over the pass right from Hazelton which is a little Indian community close to the west coast, right into the central interior.

I got a leave of absence from the company. Everyone thought I was crazy to do it. It was the middle of the winter. The temperature varied from 20 to 35 below. But I went over everybody's objections and decided I would do it on my own, without anybody helping me. I didn't want any help of planes or food or anything. No tents. Nothing. As a tribute to the Indians of this province – the first true

Canadians – I decided to revive their old trails used in the early part of the century and in the last century. They used to have a whole set of old trails blazed to communicate from Prince Rupert right into the interior.

I studied their route and set out from Hazelton three days over the mountains in extremely bad weather. After battling terrible storms at elevations of four or five thousand feet, I made it down to an Indian village. The Indians were extremely surprised to see me. The first question they asked when they knew I'd come over the mountains from Hazelton was "Where's your snowmobile?" I told them that I'd gone over the old trail. One of the young women, the only one speaking English in the whole settlement, took me to her own home and I met her mother, the daughter of the old chief of the band. She knew about the trail. Only the old people knew. It was a fantastic feast there – bannock and soup. I spent the evening with them seeing their crafts, talking to them. It was a tremendous experience.

The next day I set out again. It took me three days along the lake. I thought that trip along the lake would be an easy one. But I was wrong because the weather was so inclement. I kept remembering that I had sworn to beat the snowmobiles. I was determined to beat them. I was used to camping in groups. But camping by yourself at night was quite a different experience. You are all alone. The wolves are around you. There were two or three nights when the wolves were camping all around my campfire. The first night I hardly slept at all. Then I told myself that if I did not sleep I would not make it. So the next night I slept six hours straight.

There's a tremendous controversy about wolves in this country, but I am committed to preserving our wildlife, especially our wolves. I have a deep respect for them. They helped me out in one section of my trip. I was in the mountains following a creek and ended up in a canyon. It was deep snow and I had a 45-pound pack on my back. I found myself in front of a 200-foot waterfall. I thought I'd have to go all the way back until I found a wolf track. I followed the track and discovered that the wolf had found a way around the walls of the canyon, and I was able to climb out. It took me a few hours, but I made it without going back. This happened twice.

I planned to cover about 20 miles a day but I couldn't make it because of the weather. But on the last two days I walked a day, a night and a day steady without a stop. I didn't sleep; I only stopped to eat. I had taken dried foods, soups and meats. I felt good. Really good. Not exhausted at all. I thought I would be after 36 hours of walking straight. But I found at the end that I went really fast. As I got close to the end I saw a whole bunch of people, miles in the distance. I thought they were waiting with the snowmobilers, who were just about to start off. The first snowmobile passed me just 15 minutes before I reached my finishing line. And all the people came to me. They were waiting for me. It was amazing. It was a fantastic experience.

Fred, forester

What about our heritage?

It bugs my conscience here the way we have to work. It's not the quality of the work you do that is important, it is just how much you can get through. I find it difficult to work fast. I have been taught to do a good job, but to do it in the time that it needs to be done properly. Here, my boss just wants us to get through as many trucks as possible, even if a truck has to come back again next week for further work. I don't like that. I feel it is not a proper way to do it. I like to do a good job and know I have done it well.

When you first come here it is as if you are in a sack. You know nothing of what is going on. For a year or so, until you can read the paper or listen to the radio or TV, you have no idea what is going on anywhere. That is a thing we have learned about America. They don't care too much about what is happening in Europe, whereas in Finland, we heard the news from all over Europe. We knew what was going on in different countries, even in America. Here, all you learn about is Canada and the USA, and that's it.

I would like to feel that the children at school had a broader scope. I'd like to know they are learning more about the whole world. But here, that does not seem so important. I think the educational system is probably adequate here, but only adequate. Are the children taught ideals, strength, something of their heritage? I don't see how you can live successfully without that. Here, it all seems so different.

Heimo, mechanic

Hypocrisy

Being an immigrant in Canada is being a second-class citizen. We have to work twice as hard and be twice as good for the same job. The attitude of the Canadian authorities is very hypocritical. For instance, somebody told me that in Japan they do not allow immigrants. Well and good. They are straightforward in telling you you are not wanted. You know where you stand. But when Canada advertises about the equal opportunities here and people come because of it, why not give them a chance? If you don't need immigrants, don't invite them in.

Aslam, accountant

Very American

Little by little I began to feel free here. I was doing much the same as I had done in Spain, but I felt part of a freer society. It was a good feeling. In the beginning, this was like a revelation to me and I saw Canada as something fantastic. Then slowly, I began to see the reality of the situation. I began to see how Canada is very American and, perhaps because of my background, I reject many of these American values. But that is now after four years. In the beginning I adored it all. I was like a young bird who leaves the nest for the very first time. I was afraid but I loved my freedom without even knowing how I would use it.

Vicky, language teacher

Permission to work

As a Canadian I have looked around and tried to find something that belongs to me. But somehow I've found that as a Canadian I only have a duty. I have got nothing. I got permission to work, but Canada has shared nothing with me.

Edgar, hospital worker

Always an immigrant

Some of us never stop being immigrants. I was born here in a small eastern Ontario town. I went to the public school there. Then the war started. A lot of people became suspicious of us. They thought we were Japanese. They didn't seem able to tell the difference between Chinese and Japanese. The kids persecuted me. I hated it. I hated them. I even started to hate my parents and myself for being Chinese, for being different. It was the kind of trauma a small boy didn't get over easily. Even as a man I have never quite got over the bitterness of those years.

What does it mean to be a Canadian? I really thought it would help us to identify as a nation when we got our own flag. But are we still a colony of Britain, or have we thrown them off? And what about the U.S.? How will we throw them off? To be a true Canadian must you have white skin and big round blue eyes? When are we going to grow up?

Richard, storekeeper

VII

REFLECTIONS

26 Gisela: The time for doing is over

Some immigrants tell stories which seem to sum up and reflect particularly well the ambiguities and complexities of immigrant life in Canada. There is, for example, Gisela, a woman now in her seventies.

We spend an entire afternoon surrounded by the past. A long life, well lived. Old letters. Faded photographs. Broken promises. Impossible dreams. From a glass cabinet she takes out the painted wooden folk art she and her husband made during the Depression years.

When our long visit is over I feel stronger for having met her.

I came to Canada as an immigrant because of the First World War. We were Hungarians. But after the war, the part of Hungary where we lived was partitioned off and was given to Rumania. Life then was very difficult for us. The official language was changed. Work was a problem. I had wanted to be a teacher, but when the language changed it became almost impossible for me to continue my higher studies in this language that I knew very little. Many people who lived in this particular part of the country went back to Hungary, but the country was so poor that they had to live in wagons. It was an unhappy time for us.

We had friends in the United States. This man used to be a kind of apprentice in my father's shop and my mother looked after him as a young boy. When he first came to America we looked after his wife. So our families were quite close. They urged us to come to America saying they would help. They said they wanted to do this for us. We talked a great deal about it and made up our minds that my father was too old to come and find work here. It was decided that as I was the older girl I would have to come. I didn't want to. I didn't want to at all, but my parents said that if I wouldn't, then my younger sister must come. I loved my sister and felt I couldn't do that to her, so I made up my mind that it was my duty to my family. And I came. The year was 1925 and I was 19 years old.

By the time our friends in America sent us the money and we went to get the papers, there were already so many people leaving Rumania for the United States that the quota was filled. We were advised to try Canada. "It's not too far, and once you're there you can quite easily come over," our friends assured us.

I knew nothing about Canada at that time. When I knew I was coming I looked in my school books and found only four lines about the country. The four lines said that Canada was a dominion of England. It never told how many provinces there were or what the main cities were. None of that did I know. But there were some people from our town who had come to Canada already, so we wrote to them and they wrote back telling us it was not bad here. In any case, I thought Canada was going to be only a kind of temporary refuge for me. (It's wonderful to think that now – 50 years later!) I had no idea then that it would be impossible to go to my friends and that I would be happy to stay here.

Right from the time I first came, I liked Canada. I liked the people. It was so simple and friendly, especially after the experience where we had been despised after our own country was taken over by the Rumanians. Here, they didn't mind. They didn't laugh at us when we couldn't speak English. They were very helpful. It was a great adventure but I was so heartsick. If I had been able to come with the family it would have been different. But I was so lonely.

In Winnipeg I was met by an old couple in their seventies who had come earlier from my own hometown. The first thing was to find me a job. But of course I had known it would be hard. Before I had left my own country I had heard about those embroidery machines. I was good at hand embroidery so I went to a big city near my home to one of the big shops where they were doing this embroidery by machine. I stayed there for two weeks and paid money so that they would teach me how to do it.

In January, my friends saw an advertisement in the paper asking for a girl who knew machine embroidery. They came with me and we went down right away. The people who had advertised hardly believed that I knew about the embroidery machines. But when I sat down at one they saw that I knew more or less what I was doing. They said that they would take me on and teach me until I was more experienced and had learned some English. My pay was to be $7 a week.

These people were very good to me. I slept there on a small cot and they charged me only $2 each week for my supper. I was so happy. I worked at that same place for 20 years! It was the best thing that ever happened to me. These were the first friends I had here who really cared for me. They were young people, more or less my own age, who had been recently married. They were second generation Russians.

Now, out of those $7 that I earned, I started to pay back the money that our friends in the States had sent for my fare. It was $300 I owed them. After a few months, they wrote me a letter saying that I seemed kind of lonely and wouldn't it be better if instead of paying them back, I sent money to my sister so that she might come and join me? By the spring, my sister was here, too. I had always loved my sister, even more than I loved myself. I was full of joy. My friends in the shop told me that this was the first time they had heard me laugh.

We moved to a little room, the two of us. You know, when I think back to the things we had to live through I wonder how we had the strength to endure it. How could we have dared to come to this country without knowing the language, without any support really. Just with our own resources. My sister was an expert in dressmaking and she got a job in a dress factory as soon as she came.

I spoke a little English but not too much. We wanted to go to night school and learn the language. But if we said we could not work because we had to go to school we would have been without jobs. I have always liked to read, and gradually I learned to speak. The idea in the back of our minds always was to bring our parents out here. At the same time I had an understanding with a young man in the old country. His parents had died in the war and he became a soldier, 18 years old. After the war ended they kept him an extra three years in the army to serve his regular military service. He wanted to marry me even before I left my country. But I told him that I had already applied to come to Canada because our family had many debts and I wanted to help my father. This young man had no money of his own, so he said he would work toward coming over one day, too. We had written to each other ever since that time.

He had some difficulty with his papers. He was born on the other side of the border and there was some confusion about his being Rumanian, though he had been in the Hungarian army. It took about four years to settle this business of his citizenship. But finally, he got his passport and came to Canada to join me. At that time, Canada didn't need people in the cities. My husband had got into the country by giving $200 to the immigration office guaranteeing that he would go to a farm to work for a year. Friends who had bought a farm said they would take us as workers. My sister stayed in the city. She had a good job by then and friends, too.

We worked terribly hard. My husband didn't like the work or the life on the farm. He was a builder, a bricklayer, and he was used to earning good money. He knew nothing about horses, only a little about gardening, and he had to go out threshing. The farm food was all meat and potatoes. They would kill a pig, pour lard on it and freeze it. Then every day, every day it was this pork meat and fresh potatoes. It was all right but we were not used to it. There was no fresh fruit or vegetables. My husband became sick. By the time the really hard work began on the farm, he had lost a lot of weight.

The foreman was naturally peeved, but my husband forced himself to work, no matter how sick he felt, because he didn't want to hurt the people who had hired him.

Both of us were working. We had been promised $300 a year for my husband and $100 for me. The wheat was a very good price when we started, about a dollar a bushel. But it was 1929 and that winter the Depression came. It was the big crash. Everything went down. The farmers had a wheat pool, and the Grain Exchange would then sell their wheat. At the end of the year, they could not pay us. We had to come in to Winnipeg with no money at all. Everything was slack. There were no jobs.

My husband was ready to give up. He was easily discouraged. But I never gave up. I got a bit of work now and again at the place where I had been working before my marriage. They gave me work whenever they had any themselves. Then the Hungarian consul suggested I try making some Hungarian embroidered handicraft to sell. And then my husband started to paint. We would buy cheap wooden objects; I would draw the traditional designs and he would paint them. I learned in this period that women are stronger than men. After all, it was just as difficult for me and I had to go on, too, and do the best I could.

We had to look for the cheapest possible room and it had to be close to the centre of the town so that when I was called for work I could walk there. We got back the $200 we had put down as guarantee at the immigration office and we found a room for $10. But I didn't want to touch that $200. So if we made $3 a week, then we lived on $3. My husband would go out and find second-day bread and we didn't buy clothes.

The hardest thing for us at the time was that we were not wanted. Two young people, ready to work, and no one had anything for us to do. Then they started to give out relief, as they called it. But I was bitter. "I don't want any relief," I said. "I didn't come here to live on relief. I want to work." We lived in miserable conditions but we always had a phone so that people could phone us if there was work. That was the most important thing for us. Employers wanted only the cheapest labour they could find. Old, trusted employees were let go, and cheap casual labour got the jobs.

We lived very poorly and gradually we were persuaded to accept relief. I was crying and angry and my husband was really sore at me. "We have to live," he insisted. They gave us tickets to buy necessities. It almost killed me. I would sooner not have eaten. This went on for five years. Yes, it was five years before my husband could finally get a job. This, even though, poor man, he would get up very early each morning and go to where they had signs saying that they were taking on men. He even bought a bicycle so that he could travel far out of the city to try for work. But there was no work.

I knew that one day it would end and that we would get out of it. But it was so hard while it lasted. People today have no idea what it was like in those years from '29 to '35. It was really in 1935 that things started to improve economically. People then felt there would be a war soon, and they started to prepare for it. Having lived through a world war, as a young girl in the old country, I was interested to see now how a war started. Now again, the hatred began. Windows of German merchants were smashed. And as always in these cases, many innocent people were made to suffer.

We asked permission then to bring our parents out, but we were told we were not making enough to support them. So we tried even harder to make a little more money here and there, and finally, between myself and my husband and my sister's little family, we managed to get permission. My parent's house in Rumania was worth one fare. We sent the other fare and promised we would look after them always. They came in 1939 just as the war started. My father was now 71. He was with us until he was 82, and my mother lived on another nine years after that. Once my parents came it was easier for me. Now I could work overtime and come home and find soup ready on the table. We worked hard and at last we were able to buy a home of our own.

After the war my brother-in-law, who had known the west coast, found a job in Vancouver and come out with his family. We followed them out. We didn't want our family ever to be separated again. We all bought old houses, renovated them and repaired them. We always bought houses we could rent part of.

When I look back on it all I think it has all been worth it. My parents are buried here, so I would never dream of leaving now. My sister's children are here, too, and we could not leave them either. I loved Canada from the beginning. Maybe that's the reason I was able to adjust through all the difficulties we had. It always has seemed to me to be a very decent place. People here help each other.

But, you know, there is no end to difficulty in life. After a few years here in Vancouver working very hard, we were able to buy a lovely, big old house. We fixed it up so that it was beautiful. We had a number of nice rooms which we rented out to elderly ladies. All of them had seen better days. They were widows who had grown old and who had to live in small quarters. But then the city told us to reconvert this big house to a single family dwelling. They had built too many apartment blocks. There were empty suites so they didn't like us to be renting these little suites that were not complete. But then they brought in a new by-law so that we couldn't even make complete suites. There was no way we could keep the house then. That was in '66. We sold it and bought another little old house just for ourselves.

My husband is 77 now. He is still working but just a little bit. He feels better when he does. I can't work now. I have dizzy spells and sometimes fall, so I don't even go out too much. I think it all started from this worry when we had to sell the big house. It's too bad. I've always worked hard. And now, I think I would like a nice house for my old age. And maybe a trip back to visit Hungary. But my husband likes a very simple life. He always says, "No. We should wait." I think now the time for waiting is long past for us. Maybe even our time for doing is over, too.   Gisela, housewife

27 Kazuhiko: Families make a country

A bespectacled young man in blue striped overalls. "A janitor must wear a uniform. It looks professional," he explains. He chain smokes and radiates an intense, nervous energy. His youth is a sharp contrast to the sense of history which pervades his thinking and his life.

There was an Olympic in Munich five years before I came here. I had never heard that word "Munich" before, but with the Olympics Munich became very close to me. I found out where the next Olympic was going to be held and I came to Canada. I wanted to be here for the festival itself, and I thought that maybe some kind of communication might be needed between Canada and Japan for the Games. I was a writer in Japan. I made TV and radio programmes. I did all sorts of jobs. Sometimes, I worked as a plumber. But my main job was always writing.

There was a magazine series in Japan on human beings. It was a featured series in one of the well known women's magazines. They did stories on interesting couples. There was a story about a Japanese couple in Edmonton who had a bean curd store. A very interesting couple. So when I came to Canada I went to Edmonton to see this couple for a radio show I was doing. I stayed there for one month. For me, Edmonton was a very interesting town. It was my first time outside Japan. The sun seemed so big in Edmonton. It made the sun in Japan seem very small. I travelled all around the area and met an immigrant girl who was very lonely and sick. She was Japanese and could not speak English very well. She was heartbroken over a romance in Japan. She was not such a strong girl, but very interesting in the way she talked.

When my work was over I went back to Japan. But now I had a strong pull to come back to Canada. Canada was a very big image for me. Then this girl came back to Japan, too. We met again and we lived together and loved for one year. We came back to Edmonton then and got married there. Then we came to Vancouver.

I decided that the Japanese community needed a bookstore and I made plans to open one. It was 1971 and I knew no one in Vancouver. I didn't have much money, either. Just $40. So I went downtown. I wasn't afraid. I can live anywhere. I always think you need only one of three points to succeed. Hard work, money or head power. Now, for instance, I am a janitor. I have no money, my head power is very low but I do hard work. But at that time when I first arrived, I came with lots of head power.

I leased a store in Powell Street. My books were coming from Japan but the doors of the store were not yet open. Not on the front side. Not on the back. I was very, very angry because I had already paid. It seemed there was somebody living inside. I knocked and knocked but there was no answer. Just sometimes a cat would meow. Finally I brought my friend, a strong man, and he kicked in the door. There was a very heavy smell there – mess and stuff everywhere, because the cats couldn't go outside. And there was an old man sleeping.

He smiled a very weak smile when he saw me. Not a laugh. Just a weak smile. I could not speak English at that time. I could only look him in the face. But he was sick and his legs were swollen. He was undernourished. He had been drinking nothing but alcohol. He was afraid I was going to throw him out because he could not pay rent. And it was an area of the city where you were not allowed to live. He had just got in there and started to live in my store.

The only English I knew was "How do you do?" So I said that the first time and he replied "How do you do?" too. I could not speak any more. If he had been a strong guy, I would have thrown him out. But he was not. The next time my wife and I came we brought a lunch and supper. After maybe two weeks, we talked to him. It took a long time because we had no language. It was like Helen Keller. Very difficult. But I understood his mind and he understood mine. He said, "You must open your bookstore, because your books are already coming from Japan." By then he was already a little bit better. His health had grown stronger because he had been eating.

He was a carpenter and a plumber and he could do a lot around the place to help me. But he said that if I made him move he would not have a home. He suggested I make a small store in the front and let him live in the back. Now, my store was very long. He made a very small store just in the front, and he lived in the back with his four cats. It was a very good idea. I had leased a very big place, but I had a very small bookstore. There was such a heavy smell there from the cats that the customers were always like this. *(He holds his nose and laughs.)* Finally I asked him to move to my home.

He was very funny about a trunk that he had had for a long time. He had a very important key to lock it. He kept everything in this trunk – mainly old newspapers, not so important, I think – but he always kept it locked with the key. He came with his trunk to live in my home. Now I could use all my store. In the mornings we would go to the store to work. We had no money, of course. He did all the work free. And he had lots of nails and tools. Anyway, the bookstore at last looked like a real store.

This old man lived with us and every night we would have long discussions. Little by little, his health grew stronger. He had great intelligence. He knew all about Canada and many times he helped me. For instance, sometimes the lights would be turned off. I would look at my neighbour, and his lights would be on. Just the lights in my store would be off. I could not read English, but Gordon, the old man, could tell me that the letters said I must pay my bills before they would turn the lights back on.

We helped each other. We had a little boy, my wife and I. Gordon was like a grandfather to him. It was all very natural. Even now, we have been living together for four years and I still don't

209

know his middle name or where he was born or anything about his family. Once he told me he came out here to Vancouver on the top of a train from Montreal. But I don't know when. Maybe he told me but I couldn't understand. I only understand about 10 per cent or 12 per cent of what he says. He doesn't have any teeth. So it is very difficult to understand. But now he is a part of my family. I think that a family is a thing like that.

Four years is very short, but it is very long, too. Now, after four years together, funny things happen. At home we always speak Japanese. Sometimes we talk English but Gordon understands 80 per cent of what we say anyway. I forget he speaks English. Sometimes my wife says that dinner is ready. She says it in Japanese and very naturally he answers "yes." That's very simple, of course. But even deeper things, he understands. Even if we are talking Japanese he sometimes will break in and comment on the same subject. It is very, very funny. I can't understand it.

The bookstore did not go well. I could understand the mind. I could not understand the economy. It is a very important thing. But after that, I had a gift shop. The next time, in Pacific Centre, I opened a fur shop. But my business grew too fast. I had just $40, a big bank loan and a lot of trouble. I had to close. I went bankrupt. Now I owe a lot of money. I had this bad accountant who used to write all the cheques. Of course I had to check the books, but I didn't understand anything. It doesn't matter. Losing is the knife with two edges. If one side doesn't cut, you use it as a stick. Then you must try the other side.

I went back to Japan after I went bankrupt. I did horse racing, bicycle racing, every kind of gambling. I was drinking. Everything was gone. When I came back here we could not even buy a diaper for my baby. This past summer I sold all the furniture, the TV – everything. By the end of the year I had nothing in my home. Just a bank loan. I looked for a job but I didn't speak English. Then I started to think.

Big cities have many townhouses. Many townhouses have active people – husband and wife who both work. These people need a housekeeper, but they cannot afford it because the townhouse is too small. That was my idea. I would be a housekeeper. Not by the day or by the hour. Just by the job! If a housekeeper comes in she takes all day. But some jobs I can do in one hour. Now I have seven customers that I do in one day. I do floors, windows, vacuuming – everything. I am very tired each day. It is a lot of work. But I do a good job.

I want to become number one in my job. It is very easy to be number five or number ten. But to be number one you must have an actor's sense. A janitor's job looks very simple – it's just cleaning. But it is more than that. You must please the customer. Think of a hairdresser. If a customer goes to a hairdresser and gets a bad cut, it's a bad job. But if the customer likes it, then the hairdresser is considered to have a very high technique. A janitor's job is the same thing. We all wear the same overalls. We all must get down on our knees. *(At this point he gets down on his knees to demonstrate what he means.)* Now, most people do their cleaning this way with their heads down. *(He acts out what he is saying.)* But I know that eyeline is most important. Look at the difference if I keep my back straight and my eyeline level. It is very important. That's something I learned when I was a TV producer.

My wife always stays home because that makes good children. I don't worry about my wife. If a woman wants a stable job then she chooses that. My wife chose me. I have my ups and downs. Maybe it's hard for her, I don't know. The life of an immigrant is always hard.

Canada is a young country. It needs older style. My heart is young, I have young children, I have young lifestyle, but my home has a long history. Gordon has a good history, too. A long history. He knows how to make history and that's very important. A young man has energy but he does not know how to make dreams. He needs a teacher. Canada is like that. It is a young country. It needs teachers. It needs immigrants from old countries like England, like Japan and other countries with long traditions. They will bring some bad customs, too. That must be. Right now, Canada wants just good customs. It is not possible. Each family has its own customs and philosophy, and all together, all those families make a country.

Kazuhiko, janitor

28 Einar:
Part and parcel
of Canada

This tall, scraggy man with a hawk-like nose is vitally interested in history. Especially the history of the Lakehead region. He spent five weeks of his holidays last summer looking through microfilm of old newspaper clippings. And it is all there in his head. "We could have talked for 10 hours," he tells me. As we talk he doesn't look at me. He just puts his head back, closes his eyes and remembers.

There is a lot of confusion about the reason for immigration. Sure immigrants are needed to build up the country. That is true as far as it goes. But I think the business community wanted immigrants for something else completely. They wanted immigrants for cheap labour and, of course, to break the land on the prairies. Nobody can deny that. And it's still the same thing today.

I was a farmer in the old country. The farm had been in the family for eight or nine generations and had continued to be divided among the sons. Finally, it came to the time when there was not much left. I decided to come here to stay for a few years and earn enough money to pay off my brothers and sister and at least accumulate a bit more land. It was the custom practised in all of Europe. But it didn't always work out that way. At that time the Depression was in full swing in Canada. I'd seen in the papers a lot of talk about "depression" but I didn't even know what that was. I had the idea that anyone who wanted to work could always work. Depression – I didn't fall for that.

Six of us came. My neighbour had a brother who was working in B.C. in railroad construction. He convinced our neighbour to come and to bring another five guys with him. We came to Nelson, B.C. My God, Nelson was flooded with unemployed. At that time, the railroad going west stopped at Courtney Landing and they took the passengers to Proctor on boats with a big wheel at the back. Then the railroad continued on from Proctor to Nelson. We got into Nelson on a Sunday night. We were something unusual. They could see we were all dressed up and they couldn't figure out why. Everybody stopped and stared at us.

We were met by my neighbour's brother and next day we had to turn round and go back to Proctor and then go 50 miles by boat on Courtney Lake. When we came into the work camp I thought I'd reached the end of the road. Here was a little tent. It was around nine in the evening. I hadn't shaved for weeks and weeks. I was filthy. And what a reception! It seems that in the first place this guy had no right to ask us to come, and this caused quite a commotion. Some guy went into the office to tell the contractor what had happened. Next there comes a guy swearing and raving, and this is what he said. It was my introduction to Canada. He said, "Put the bastards to work. If they are workers keep them, if they are no good, to hell with them."

We were 30 miles out in the wilderness. There was no life, no community. We were cheated right and left. Even the clerk in the office took $5 poll tax from us. We told some other guys about it and they laughed. Single men used to have to pay $5 poll tax each year. But here, there was no community, there was nothing. And we were the only guys had to pay poll tax. But what could we say? We were scared anyway to say anything, in case we were laid off. That was the wild west, if ever it existed anywhere.

Mostly, the guys that were used building those railroads got nothing. About a mile from this place where we worked was a gang of 17 or 18 guys. Scandinavians they were, all expert railroad constructors. They worked for 15 months, cleaning out a huge moun-

214

tain, and when they were finished and the engineer came to give them their kill, they had nothing coming. They'd worked 15 months and all they had were their working clothes!

We worked for something like 35 cents an hour. We made about $3 a day. But the bunkhouse cost $1.50 a day. I was too young to think much in those days. And these old railroad construction workers I was with were a bit like poker players. It was a gamble. They went in to these things always feeling that if their luck held out they would make a stake. Sometimes they made a little, but most times not. Sometimes you were out a few months, sometimes a year or more. The winters were hard. You lived in tents with the wood stove going 24 hours a day. And you better make sure the stove is going!

We stayed there a few months until the railroad was finished. Then I went with a gang to Penticton, B.C. Again on railroad construction. I left the West then and set out for Hamilton, Ontario where I had friends. But I stopped over in Port Arthur to see some guys I'd gone to school with. When I met them I decided to stay on with them. You might say I'm still on my way to Hamilton. *(He laughs.)*

I rode the freight from Penticton. Every railroad freight coming east or going west was so full of unemployed . . . and they have long freights out on the prairies because the land is flat. The tops of the cars were so crammed, there was hardly even a spot where there was room for another extra guy. But that's how I came here. I had only about $125 and it would have been foolish to buy a ticket.

There was no work here. My God, I couldn't even explain what the city was like then with unemployed. You would have had to see it to believe it. Port Arthur was a centre for hundreds of thousands of bush workers – single men, the majority of them Finnish. When there was no bush work, then you had some four or five thousand bush workers beside the other unemployed. When I came here in 1931 there was no bush work, and you could hardly walk on the sidewalk. And by that time, the Port Arthur people had stopped looking for work. If you were to say to someone you were going down to the employment office, they'd think there was something wrong with your head. They'd have laughed, because there was nothing there.

They started the Trans-Canada highway then and I worked on that for some time. But between 1931 and 1936, I worked very, very little. And there were hundreds of people that worked even less. I didn't have time to get demoralized, though. I could hardly talk any English but I got mixed up with the rest of the unemployed movement, so it was a struggle for life. There were demonstrations, meetings, planning for the next day to try to get relief and so on. You never really had time to stop to think about yourself. For people who were not so involved, it was hard. Some people ended up in the mental institutions, a lot ended up in the sanitoriums, some committed suicide.

Port Arthur was not an industrial city. There was no such thing as an industrial working class. There were a few paper mills but they were closed tight, too. For some reason terrific resentment had been built up here against foreign-born people. So you heard that all day long. "You God-damn foreigners, why don't you go back to where you came from?" I must say, for quite some time, foreign-born people here, we became very anti-British. In the first place you saw British people, the few that worked. Of course there were lots that couldn't, but the foremen were Scottish, the police were Scottish and so on. And for a while, we thought of course that all the British, all the Scotsmen, were working. But when you had meetings with the rest you found out that a lot of them were English-speaking people. For a time I was anti-British, but I realized after a while that that was being foolish, so I quit that lonely view. Then we came to the Second World War and all of a sudden, everyone realized we were all in it together. Since the war, I've never heard anything about "God-damn foreigners" or anything like that any more.

I'm not bitter. In fact I'd say I've had a damn good schooling. And it's done me a lot of good. When I came here some of my old friends used to say, "I'd rather work for an English-speaking foreman than for my own nationality." I couldn't understand that. It took me time. You see, when an immigrant comes here he tries his damnedest to work for a particular foreman if he is from his own country. He has a feeling that they are the same nationality and he'll be treated better.

But that was where immigrants made their biggest mistake. When it comes down to real exploitation, nobody can exploit a Finn as much as a Finnish contractor or a Finnish foreman. And the same thing goes for all the rest of nationalities. Like the Swedish contractor who was able to prevent his bush workers from organizing for the simple reason that they were mostly Scandinavian immigrants who had just come here. He paid them much less than what the rest were paid. After they'd been here for a few months and learnt to speak a little, they found out they'd been cheated. But by then he'd brought in a fresh load of people!

There's no doubt there is a political policy here to keep the nationalities divided. You've got the Finns; they have their community here and they get grants to do this and this. The Ukrainians do the same. The Swedes the same. And so on. Then you have politicians who try to play one against the other. Very often, it's hard for a worker to see through this kind of thing.

I always remember the advice that Karl Marx gave German emigrants. He told them not to try to take their country with them but to learn the ways of where they were going, to learn the language and become part and parcel of that country's working class if they wanted to make a good living there. I think that advice still holds true today.

Einar, bus driver

Conclusion:
We made this country
live and grow

A country of immigrants. A great country. But it has cost a lot to make it what it is. Some were destroyed in the process. Some refused to give in. All have earned their stake in the land.

Older, quieter, smaller

I was only two years old when I came here. Didn't remember anything of the old country. I just know that from ever since I can recall my old man used to talk about the old days. What it was like in the village where we came from. He never shut up about the house we lived in, or the farm he used to share with his brother, or the time he was elected president of the local club or some organization they used to have for dances and debates and stuff like that. I never paid too much attention to him.

To tell you the honest truth, by the time I was about six or seven years old, I hardly could speak to my father. He more or less still spoke Italian, and more or less I spoke English. But we didn't have a language in common. And as the years went by it got worse. Aw, he spoke a bit of English. But just what he had to learn for his job as a maintenance man in a big factory where they made plastic toys. It was an okay job and he could get by with just a bit of English because most of the other guys there also were foreigners.

I spent as much time as I could away from home playing pool with my friends or hockey or just bumming around at some other kid's house. Wasn't that I didn't care about my parents, but it was like as if we were from different families. I mean, we didn't have anything in common. I mean, it was as if they just sort of came here but stayed in Italy at the same time. Do you know what I mean? My father would shoot it off all the time about his village back home and how great it used to be and what a big shot he was there, but it was almost like he didn't live here at all. He wasn't living his life in the present. There was no present for him. Just the past. The past and maybe the future. I think he always expected that somehow one day the future would turn into the past again and he'd be someone important again.

Anyway, when I was 18 he took me on a visit back to Italy. To be honest, I wasn't mad about going. But on the other hand he was paying the whole trip and it was a good holiday. I had just quit school and didn't have a job yet or anything. Nothing steady. And to tell the truth, I guess I was a bit curious about my father. Like I wanted to know just who this man really was.

But wow, we get to my father's village and it is like nobody's ever seen him before. Oh sure, there was his sister and her husband. But hardly anyone else. You see, this village of my father's is really, really small and 16 years have passed since he left there. So some people have died, others have moved out. And all that. It didn't seem like too many people knew him anymore. And when he takes me one day to where this big farm is he had with his brother, it's like a big garden. I wouldn't ever call it a farm.

That trip was a disaster for my father. It was like his memory was playing a dirty trick on him. When we came back home he was sort of older, quieter, even smaller in a way. It was almost as if he didn't care anymore. Even my sister could do what she wanted and he didn't seem to notice if she was home or not. Then my mother died just a few months later and my dad just folded up like he was finished. He didn't die or anything, but he just doesn't seem to have an interest in living any more.

Tony, truckdriver

There's got to be more to life

Sure, I've got a nice house here, a big car. In my own country I only could afford a motorbike. But so what? There's got to be more to your life than that. No one here cares too much about other people. It is very much a land where you say, "This is my business, don't you interfere. That is your business over there." Everyone has his own house, his own car, his own family. The idea seems to be you don't ask or tell or share. It's a no-no. After a while, you stop relying on your friends. You stop even asking of your family. You don't want to put them out. You don't want to cause them any trouble.

Tomas, plumber

No going back

Maybe it was only luck I came here. Luck, fate, destiny. Maybe it was the dream inside me. At best it was a fluke. I wanted to go to Australia. No way. The White Australia policy made that continent a closed shop. So it had to be Canada. It had to be. Australian racist policy made my choice for me. There was no such restriction here. The Canadian way was open and humanitarian. People were people in Canada. An equal chance for all. My dream took real shape then.

But my dream shattered into a million pieces. Not all at once, mind you. Slowly. Very slowly. Step by step. Because when the dream is big inside you, it does not shatter easy. It took me six or seven months to realize I would get no job here in any legal office as I had in my own country. Then it took another few months to face that I would get no job here in any office at all. I had to live. My wife and baby had to have food and a roof over their heads. So I took first a temporary job, cleaning corridors in a hospital. Endless corridors. You cleaned them even when they were not dirty. It was not such a hard job. What was hard was the way I was treated by people. I ceased to be a real person, someone other people might say "hello" to as they went past. I became much like the mops and the brooms I used. I was another cleaner. Just another Filipino cleaner.

The money I earned didn't make the way I was treated any easier to take. So I quit after I managed to get a job as a security guard. I exchanged my mops for a uniform but it hasn't helped me much. I am still the "little Filipino guy" as I heard someone call me the other day.

My dream now is gone. What is this Canada people talk about? This just, equal place where people enjoy a multicultural society? It is a sham, no better than a White Australia. Worse really for being hypocritical. I laugh when they speak of no racial prejudice here. It is so strong here that they see you coming up the street and have you all typecast by your colour, before they even see the features of your face. I am here because there is no going back for me. But I am a disillusioned man.

Philip, security guard

In limbo

I feel very much in limbo. Every day is a new trial. Every morning you must start again. I want to see it this way. I know that my children here will start a brand new life. I must try to believe it has been worth it.

Eichi, TV repairman

Damn good Canadians

The immigrants to this country, we done the dirty work that made it live and grow. We worked where there was somethin' to be done. We bust our guts plantin' and pickin'. We went loggin' in the bush, sluggin' down trees and haulin' them to where they had a use. We did everythin' in our day. I'm not kiddin' you. My God, the woman lives next door to me, 'er grandmother came to this country as a young woman. She was a real service to the country, that lady. Yes, sir. She was a – a – (*He laughs and shakes his head.*) I dunno what you'd call 'er exactly, but she was a lady well known in these parts. Worked like blazes they say and made 'er own little pot up 'ere. There weren't many women could take it up 'ere in those early days. I never knew 'er myself, but they say she was one hell of a woman. Got grandchildren all over the province. And damn good Canadians they are, too. Yes, sir. No way Canada could 'ave got by without 'er immigrants. And that goes for today as well.

Alfred, logger